This book is so relational in every aspect of a police wife's life. Hearing all the stories from other police wives really brings to life how our lives are so challenging and rewarding at the same time.

Jessica Garland
Founder, Wives Behind the Blue
Mt. Sterling, Kentucky

This book will help all of us. It's definitely something that is needed.

Jennifer Foster
Treasurer, Blue Line Wives

Really good book. *Wives Behind the Blue* gives you a great beginning point to understanding the life wives of Officers lead and promotes great comraderie! I Would recommend it to be at the top of the gift list for new Police Wives.

Kelli Lowe
President, National Police Wives Association

WIVES BEHIND THE BLUE

Published by WordCrafts Press
Cody, Wyoming 82414
www.wordcrafts.net

WIVES
BEHIND
THE BLUE

MONICA AMOR

WordCrafts

Contents

THIS BOOK IS DEDICATED

To all the beautiful, faithful, courageous, loving wives behind the blue. You have been given a high calling, and yes, at times it's hard, but know that you are not alone.

"The thin blue line: A symbol of heroism, not corruption."

The thin blue line represents a stance that we are all in this together as protectors of our citizens. The alternative interpretation is just noise."

~ *Ed Flosi, Retired Police Sergeant*

So speak encouraging words to one another. Build up hope so you'll all be together in this, no one left out, no one left behind. I know you're already doing this; just keep on doing it.

~1 Thessalonians 5:11

A SPECIAL THANKS

I would like to say a special thank you to Allison Uribe, author of *Cuffs and Coffee*, Kristi Neace, author of *Above the Fray* and Adam Davis, author of *6 Traits of a Bulletproof Police Marriage*.

These three contributing authors make it their mission to support Law Enforcement families, helping them grow emotionally, mentally and spiritually through their various books, articles, blogs, speaking engagements and more.

The words they share through the articles they contributed for this book are filled with hope, wisdom and encouragement. It has been my complete privilege to connect with them through this project and get a glimpse of their genuine hearts for helping blue line families everywhere.

WHY WIVES BEHIND THE BLUE?

M y day job is being a lunch lady at a Military School for Junior High and High School students and while there is a chance that I may be just a wee bit biased, I happen to think being a lunch lady, particularly to these students, is one of the best jobs ever. Serving a bunch of hungry kids a warm breakfast or lunch, offering them a smile, sharing a word of encouragement and just loving on them for the few moments they pass by my cafeteria window before heading to class is a daily ministry opportunity that God has blessed me with and one I am extremely grateful for.

One very nice perk to working for a school besides building a great rapport with some amazing young people throughout the year is that just like the students, I get summer vacation. So as you can imagine, the moment the Spring season hits, the countdown for a two and a half month Summer break for students and staff begins.

During this years countdown, I began to think about how I would like to spend my summer. I knew my son would have most of the summer off from college so I wanted to make sure I had a few fun ideas in motion so we could have plenty of fun together.

The first item on my summer-to-do list was $5 Tuesday's

at the local movie theater. No matter what else we planned for summer break, I knew Tuesday's would be reserved for my son and I seeing some sort of movie. Whether it was a blockbuster hit, a cheesy B-movie or a foreign film with subtitles that we had never heard of, at only $5 per ticket it really wouldn't matter.

After $5 Tuesday, my summer wish list included ideas such as fishing, visiting historical parks and towns nearby, browsing clothing stores, bookstores, old-school record shops, a day at the beach, bowling, swimming at the gym (notice I didn't saying working out at the gym) and last but not least, one of my favorites, trying new restaurants in the area.

Feeling good about the potential summer activities I would do with my son, I thought it might be nice to also add some designated writing time to my personal list of things to do.

It had been three years since the release of my last book, and since then I had only written a handful of articles for magazines and newspapers. With summer coming and the freedom of extra time on my hands, it only seemed right to pray about the possibility of writing something new. So I prayed and asked God, what if any, writing assignments He might have for me to do over the summer.

When I first posed the question through a casual prayer, I didn't receive an immediate answer but what I did receive was a greater desire to seriously pray about it, and so I did. For weeks I kept seeking God with the same question: *"What if any, writing assignments do you have for me this summer?"*

One morning while going through my usual routine of getting ready for work, drinking a cup of coffee and reading my Bible, the summer writing prayer came to mind again. I put down my coffee cup and my Bible and took out a piece of paper and wrote down this question: *If I was to work on any writing this summer what would it be about?* I then jotted down the first three things that came my mind.

1. Write an article geared toward helping Junior High and High School age kids to grow in their faith.
2. Contact a few known magazine editors, see what articles they are looking for, write a few and then submit them for possible publication.
3. Write a book geared toward encouraging Law Enforcement Wives.

As I looked over the list, let me tell you exactly what went through my mind and how my thought process went:

God hasn't given me clear direction yet on writing this summer but if I had to choose one, I think I would like to go for writing something that could help Junior High and High School kids. It's such a tough age and I would love to write something that lets them know that despite all their hormonal changes and teen challenges they face, they will make it through. As a matter of fact, I would like for the kids that I've bonded with this past year at the military school to know that I had written something with them in mind. I love those kids and I want them to know just how amazing they are through something I write. Yes! Writing something for Junior High and High School kids would be a great summer project.

But, if God doesn't lead me that way, I could definitely contact a few magazine editors that I know and see what they are in need of and write a few articles for them. It probably wouldn't take too much time or effort and I would enjoy it. I could write and still have plenty of time to do other things over summer vacation. Yes! Just a few faith-based articles would be the better summer project.

Hmm, writing a book for Law Enforcement Wives, well that doesn't seem realistic. I don't even know why I put that one on the list. After all, the last book I wrote was supposed to be my last book wasn't it? Now, I'm just working on articles. What could I possible share anyway? I am certainly not the poster child for Law Enforcement Wives, that would probably be a woman who knows hundreds of wives of Officers and interacts with them daily. That's not me, I only know two other wives and we've rarely talked about Law Enforcement in all the time of knowing each other. I wouldn't even know where to begin.

No! Writing something for Law Enforcement Wives would not be a good summer project. I might as well cross that one off the list. I'm sure God wants me to write something else or maybe nothing at all.

Hmm, why did I even put that down as an option? I wouldn't know where to begin or how to encourage Law Enforcement Wives. The only thing I know is that I could have used a book from Law Enforcement wives when my husband first told me he wanted to become a Police Officer years ago. I think I just better keep praying."

Basically in a matter of minutes, as I contemplated my list of writing ideas, my thought process booted out the option of writing this book because I didn't feel qualified. It didn't matter that I had been a Law Enforcement wife for seventeen years, I felt inadequate to encourage other wives because I knew I could still use encouragement. And so I tried to ignore the idea of this book and instead held on to the possibility of the first two options.

Ironically, I have had enough experience with God to

know that wherever I feel the most inadequate is usually where He ends up taking me. I tend to kick and scream a bit but each time God leads me to the place I'm most insecure about, I end up growing in my faith, standing firmer in my belief and developing a deeper understanding of who He is and how He works in my life.

But I'm getting a head of myself because in this moment as I contemplated my list, I still opted for denial in the area of writing a book geared toward helping Law Enforcement Wives. Instead I just kept asking God, *What if any, writing assignments do you have for me this summer?*

Even now as I write this, I am reminded of just how patient God is with me. I don't know about you but I am a very slow learner with God at times. I kept asking the same question, *What if any, writing assignments do you have for me this summer?* because I didn't like where God's answer was leading me but apparently God wasn't worried about it.

Denial wasn't working for me and so I decided to put out a fleece just like Gideon did in the book of Judges when God was calling him to a seemingly impossible task.

My fleece was this: If God was actually wanting me to write a book that could possibly encourage other wives of Officers, then He would have to make it clear and open a door in such away that I couldn't deny it. I wasn't going to aggressively pursue a door, God would just have to present a door to me. If not, then I would know for certain that it was all just my imagination.

Shortly after my fleece declaration, I decided to send an email to to a publisher I knew, Mike Parker. I knew that he knew the market well and would give me an honest answer to this book idea that wouldn't go away.

In my email I told Mike about the book idea and asked if in his professional opinion, he thought there was a need for such a book in the market today. Honestly, I assumed he would email in a few days letting me know that Law Enforcement Wives didn't need a book and that there was no market for it. I was certain his email would be the answer to my fleece. A confirmation that I had put this book idea on my list simply by mistake.

To my complete surprise Mike responded quickly to my email, letting me know that not only was there a market for this book but that he had seen firsthand from people he knew, just how much spouses of Law Enforcement Officers needed encouragement. If that wasn't enough, he added that as a publisher, it was a book he would definitely be interested in.

Wait? What? Did God just give me confirmation through a huge open door?

I re-read Mike's email a few times before it sunk in. There was a need for a book that could help wives of Officers and he was interested it.

It couldn't have been more plain but I wasn't ready to give up on my denial yet. I wasn't fully convinced, so I threw out another fleece and this time, I was throwing it all out on my husband.

You will understand why later in this book as to why this was an even bigger fleece than the first. One I assumed would definitely confirm my initial suspicions of me *not* writing the book.

I told my husband that I had been praying about a summer writing project and how the idea of a book for Law Enforcement Wives kept coming up. I then explained the potential open door through my publisher but how I was still praying about it because although a door opens, it doesn't always mean you automatically walk through it at that time. I told him with assurance that I still needed confirmation from God. I laid out all the information I had before my husband and then I waited. I was certain he would be resistant to this idea and was already anticipating the—Sorry God, but my husband doesn't want me to write this particular book and I know you want me to be obedient to him—speech I was going to give.

But to my complete shock, not only was my husband on board with the book idea, the tone in his voice and the look of in his eyes showed a genuine compassion for potential readers. "Wow! A book like that could really help a lot wives" he said.

Wait! What? Who is this man? What have you done with my husband?

I had thrown out two fleeces and God confirmed what He wanted me to do both times.

Now I know none of you are like this, but I still didn't surrender my denial. I opted for just one more fleece, If it really was God's will for me to put a book together over the summer for Law Enforcement Wives then I needed to feel a peace beyond all understanding.

I recruited a few prayer warriors to pray with me for clear direction and though I did not anticipate receiving a peace beyond all understanding due to my own insecurities, I did ask the prayer warriors if they happen to know of any Law Enforcement wives they could refer me just in case God revealed the crazy idea that I really was supposed to write this book. I thought if God gave me 12 potential contacts along with the peace I requested then perhaps I needed to lay down my denial once and for all. And so I prayed and waited.

Within two days my few prayer warriors sent me names of twenty-four Law Enforcement wives wanting to be a part of the project should I moved forward with it.

Still waiting for the peace beyond all understanding portion of the fleece, I sat down and wrote out a pros and cons list to writing this book, starting with the "con" side. I gave God every reason as to why I felt I was unqualified for this particular project. I thought He could probably find a Law Enforcement Wife who was much more plugged in and connected in ways that I had never been. I also included my concerns over the whole editing, marketing and promoting process that takes place, as there is so much more that goes into a book beyond just the writing. I reminded him that I was only asking for a summer project, and writing a book could take so much longer.

After completing a very long "con" list, I then went over to the "pro" side and wrote only two things:

1. When we first started this journey years ago, I could have benefited from a book that shared experiences from other wives of Officers letting me know what to expect and how to handle some of the unique situations that come from living the Law Enforcement life.
2. I think God is calling me to do this.

Only two things listed on the "pro" side but they were important ones. I sat there waiting to feel something, perhaps warm fuzzies before I actually committed to God to move forward but it just wasn't happening that way. I stared at the "pro" list for some time wondering what else I could add to it but nothing came to mind beyond what I had already listed.

It seemed like it took forever but I eventually put my pen and paper down and said out-loud, *"Alright God, I'll do it!"*

I will tell you the truth, as soon as I uttered those words out-loud a peace beyond all understanding instantly came over me. In that moment I realized that God wasn't concerned about my "con" list or with me feeling secure enough to write a perfect book, He just wanted my obedience. He wanted me to push beyond my feelings of doubt, trust Him and do what He was calling to do.

Once it was settled in my heart, the first thing I did was to take a jumbo size crayon and write these words that reflected a big part of my fears and how I needed to deal with them across my closet mirror:

Shift your focus from your performance to His presence.

This would be my mantra as I began putting this book together right up until the last letter on the last page. Unlike other books I have written, I didn't feel like I had a full understanding as to what the book would entail but I made my commitment to God so instead of worrying about my own ability or inability to perform well, I was determined to keep my focus on the presence of God and trust that He would bring together the right contributors, the right words and the right encouragement needed for wives behind the blue.

What to Expect

In this book you will find stories from eighteen different women, whose names have been changed for the sake of privacy, along with words of encouragement from a few different authors, and my own story. All the women sharing in this book are wives (or soon-to-be-) of Law Enforcement Officers who long to help other wives along the way through their own experiences. The questions I asked of these women focused on what type of expectations they had when they first learned of their husband's interest in Law Enforcement and how those expectations measured up or changed as time went on. I also asked them to briefly share a bit of the good and bad of being a Law Enforcement wife and how they have worked through various challenges. I chose these particular questions because they are the very things I needed to know early on and on occasion even now.

As you will see, many of the wives have similar experiences, yet their approach, mindset or viewpoints vary. I personally have found this particularly helpful in my own role as an Officers wife. To learn that another wife has gone through the exact same thing but has dealt with it differently, leading to different results is honestly helpful. Recognizing and clearly understanding many of the similarities these women have experienced has stirred a sense of sisterhood within me that really wasn't there before.

If you are a wife of an Officer and have a strong circle of other Law Enforcement wives around you then you know what it feels like to have support from other sisters. But if you are more like I was, having no circle at all, I am certain that you will find the support you need through the wives behind the blue that share a bit of their experiences with you through this book.

A WIFE'S ADVICE

Each woman in this book could easily write a more in depth personal story of their own based on their various experiences thus far, but for now what they share is a bit of both sides to what it is like for them as wives of Law Enforcement Officers. Along with their experience, the women in this book also offer a bit of insight and advice to other wives of Officers in hopes of helping them as they walk out their most incredible calling of being a wife behind the blue.

With a few of the wives offering somewhat similar advice, I initially wondered if it would come across a bit repetitive for readers but then I realized something. If a number of these strong, beautiful wives have shared similar advice that helped them succeed throughout their years as police wives then perhaps reiterating their advice to wives reading this book, including those just starting out in this special role is exactly what is needed for their success as well.

A WIFE'S PRAYER

At the end of each women's story you will find, *A Wife's Prayer*. Because this book was written for the purpose of connecting and encouraging wives of Officers in general not just for Christian Law Enforcement wives, I wasn't sure initially if including a wife's prayer was the right way to go. I didn't want some wives who may be in a different place spiritually speaking to shy away from relating to other wives in this book and gleaning from their wisdom simply because a prayer was included. But as I said from the start, *Wives Behind the Blue* is definitely a God thing. So the more I thought about it and reflected on my own experiences, and the experiences of the many wives in this book, there was no way I could deny that prayer has been a big part of the journey. Prayers offered on behalf of our husbands, children, family and ourselves. Prayers covering health, safety, wisdom, direction, forgiveness, disappointments and even the need for sanity have been a vital part of the journey for so many Law Enforcement wives.

Even if prayer wasn't what they were used to prior to their husband getting involved in Law Enforcement, something about seeing their husband put on their badge, kissing them goodbye as they head out for their extraordinarily challenging job of enforcing the law with both good and bad people, not knowing what the day may hold for them, has lead many wives to their knees.

So yes, *A Wife's Prayer* is included at the end of each wives story and is meant to be a starting point of conversation with God about your Officer and your role as his wife should you choose to pursue it.

MY THOUGHTS

The final section of each chapter, *My Thoughts* is where you the reader can write down your personal thoughts, desires, ideas or notes as to what you have learned from your blue-sisters experience, the advice she offers or the prayer that is shared. In other words, *My thoughts i*s just for you, beautiful blue sister to pour out your heart.

RESOURCES

I like to consider myself a pretty tuned-in type of person. I don't have to know it all, but I certainly like to stay up to date with a variety of things as I admit, it makes me feel young and hip to do so. As I will explain further in my own story of being a wife of an Officer, I was fully unaware of any resources available to me when my husband first entered into Law Enforcement seventeen years ago. I had no idea that I might need resources and support let alone that any was out actually there. Now with the internet, social media and my personal favorite Google, I have discovered that there are plenty of resources available to help women grow, connect and succeed as wives of Law Enforcement Officers.

Some people may think that a list of resources is only needed when or if you are having some sort of trouble but that's not true at all. If I've learned anything from this process of meeting other Law Enforcement wives, hearing their stories and putting this book together, it's that having a wealth of resources to turn to helps to keep you out of the potential self-pity party that can and does take place for a wife of an Officer who may lack supportive resources in a time of need.

At the end of this book I have listed a number of resources that I believe are useful for wives of Officers but in no way is this list limited. If you don't find a resource or two that fits your need, then by all means, go crazy on Google and find others.

My Story

For the first two years of dating and then the next ten years of marriage, my husband was a Fed-Ex guy. Working for Federal Express had been a wonderful experience for him as he enjoyed his position, his route, his shift and being somewhat of a modern-day Santa Claus delivering presents wherever he went. He also very much appreciated the stability and excellent benefits the company had to offer which allowed him to provide well for his family. As for me, I admired him and all the hard work I knew he did. And truth be told, even after so many years, my heart would still turn to mush whenever I would see him in his cute blue shorts and matching collared shirt before heading out to drive his big white truck around town delivering hundreds of priority packages to residents and businesses alike. I would feel such a sense of pride whenever we would run into the customers he delivered packages too regularly. They would always make a point to say hello to him and then would look at me and tell me how professional, kind, hard-working and wonderful they thought he was. More than once a customer would say that my husband was their favorite Fed-Ex Guy and I had to agree with them because he was my favorite too.

One of the many fantastic benefits of working for Federal

Express at the time, was that they paid for their employees college education. As long as an employee maintained a certain grade point average and passed all of his or her classes, Fed-Ex would reimburse all money spent toward earning a degree. My husband was well aware that most companies did not offer that type of benefit and therefore was eager to take advantage of the opportunity. He went to school part-time to pursue an Administrative Justice degree while working full-time and still being mindful of keep his wife and children very happy.

His days were long and often challenging to balance but he was motivated by the fact that he would be the first one in his family to earn a college degree. It took over ten years to earn his bachelors as a part-time student but earn it he did and we couldn't have been more proud.

Having reached his goal, the plan then was to pursue a career though Federal Express in investigations but as my husband began to actually look into the details of the position, speaking with different people in the department, he came across an irony that completely changed the course of his life. In order to work as an investigator for Federal Express he had to have a college degree, which he did, and Law Enforcement experience, which he did not.

If he had been able to gain the experience needed on a part-time basis while continuing his work for Fed-Ex, he would have stayed with the company and more than likely it would have been a smooth transition. But the irony of it all was that the only way he could actually gain the required Law Enforcement experience needed for an investigator position within Federal Express was to actually leave Federal Express and join the Police Academy.

This was no easy decision for my husband as he is the kind of man who is bent on security and stability at all costs. He longed to use his Administrative Justice degree to pursue a higher position within the company that had been his stability for over thirteen years, the company that supplied him with good pay, great benefits and had paid for his college education. If he left this secure job to enter the Police Academy and passed he knew he would receive greater pay and even better benefits in time but the dark cloud hanging over his head was, what if he didn't pass? Then what? No Law Enforcement job, no Fed-Ex job and no security for his family.

In retrospect, my husband realizes now that had he not passed the Police Academy, he could have reapplied at Federal Express if need be and as a previously valued employee, he more than likely would have been re-hired quickly. However, at the time, it felt like an all or nothing career move and so we did the only thing we knew to do and that was to pray for direction.

I couldn't imagine that my Fed-Ex guy would come up with this crazy idea of being an Officer on his own so I assumed right from the start that this idea was from God. I prayed that God would confirm it by opening doors for my husband and sure enough, one slow step at a time, He did. From a kind recruiter to our oldest daughters Sunday School teacher, my husband found encouragement and support to move forward through the application process of one of the most difficult Police Academy's noted in the state.

I continued to pray for opened doors and felt a sense of excitement as my husband filled out endless paperwork, passed the written exam, a strenuous physical test, cleared the drug and alcohol test and passed an intense psychological evaluation after receiving thumbs up on his character from various references. With every application requirement addressed and peace that God was in control, there was nothing left to do but wait.

I still remember the day, months after the application process began, when my husband called me and with a quiet, almost disbelief sound in his voice said, "I've been accepted to the Police Academy."

I knew he was nervous about the transition but also knew he had worked so very hard to get to this place of opportunity. We both believed without a doubt that God had opened a door for this new chapter in his life and were both willing to step through the door.

When we hung up the phone, I remember feeling overwhelmed with joy and gratitude over the fact that God would call my husband to such an honorable position. Immediately I pictured him being a leader in Law Enforcement, a person who would guide others headed down a wrong path toward a better way. He would enforce the law with integrity and fairness and would make a difference. And I pictured myself right by his side, supporting him, his career and what I considered deep down to be some sort of a future, mutual ministry. In those few moments after receiving the call that confirmed my husbands new career choice, I pictured the best of the best—and then the Police Academy began.

One of the reasons I felt so unqualified to put this book together initially was because I now know, after many years, that I had on a pair of rose-colored glasses the day I received my husband's call about being accepted to the Police Academy. As a matter of fact, I had rose-colored glasses on about many things including my young faith-walk with God.

I was a fairly new Christian learning about God's character and what it meant to walk with Him and learn from His Word one day at a time. In one way this was great because I literally believed God for every possible thing as my husband transitioned from Fed-Ex guy to Academy recruit. The downside however, of being young and inexperienced in faith was that I was under the impression that as a praying and believing Christian, I wouldn't go through too much hardship or frustration because God was on my side. With that mindset, I felt totally prepared for my husband's Law Enforcement career, starting with the 28-week Academy training.

The very first thing the kids and I did as my husband prepared for his first day at the Academy was make a chain of badges. We traced out twenty-eight Sheriff badges on light green paper and taped them on a long string. We hung the chain of paper badges on the wall with the badge at the bottom of the string having the number "1" on it, representing week one of the Academy. Each Friday we planned to tear off one badge until we reached the final badge. The number "28" badge had a tiny blue plastic Officer attached to it which was meant to be an inspirational encouragement for my husband and one small way the kids and I could be a part of what he was about to get into.

As I hung up the chain of badges vertically on our kitchen wall, I viewed it with my rose colored glasses and saw nothing but smooth sailing success, pride, and honor for my husband and for our family. I was certain that each badge we tore off would mean another level of growth and goodness for all of us through this experience.

On the first day of the Academy my husband came home completely overwhelmed. He explained how when we he walked into the classroom, each desk had dozens of books stacked high toward the ceiling as if to intimate the recruits, which indeed it did. The recruits were then informed of the various things that could get them dismissed from the Academy such as absences as well as needing to pass their weekly tests by a certain percentage. Each recruit would be given only two chances at falling below the required percentage, if there was a third fail, they would automatically be removed from the program without any questions.

It was only his first day and I knew he just needed time to adjust so I did all the good wifely things. I made him extra yummy food, listened to him, encouraged him, reminded him that he could do it and prayed for him with complete assurance as he went on his way the next day and the day after and the day after that. By the end of the first week, the first round of tests were given. My husband along with most of the recruits passed the tests but a few didn't. It was just the first week so there wasn't much concern, yet.

My husband was a bit on edge but still okay as we removed the first badge and celebrated that there were only twenty-seven more weeks to go. Then came the second and third week of tests and suddenly some recruits who were there one day, were dismissed the next. That's when it became real.

Because of his desire to always do his very best and the added "all or nothing" burden he put upon himself in regards to pursuing Law Enforcement, things became very intense, very quickly. The idea of not passing a test and being dismissed became an all consuming concern for him as well as for the other Recruits. As the weeks went by and the pressure magnified, my rose colored glasses began to slide down my nose just a bit.

I believe in my husband, I believe he is the kind of man that will succeed at anything he sets his mind too and I believed it wholeheartedly then as well, only I wasn't understanding the pressure he was putting on himself not to fail.

But it became a little more clear to me after the first month or so of paper badges removed. We found it necessary to increase our income a bit, so I took a second part time job in the evenings at a bookstore. While my husband was very appreciative of my willingness to work an additional job, it was a reminder of the security he gave up in order to pursue something he didn't have yet. If he passed the Academy he knew he would have a good career and could provide very well for his family but if he didn't...that was the burden.

With me taking on an evening job, our oldest daughter, just coming into her teen years, stepped up in responsibility and helped with her younger siblings as well as around the house. Though it was a good thing and did help my husband to remember that we were all in this together, the responsibility shifts and the new Academy routine started to take it's toll.

My husband was gone all day and I worked at night so the weekends quickly became our only real time to spend together if at all, as studying naturally took priority. Although our kids were excited to support their dad and help him pull off one paper badge after another as the weeks passed by, they also really missed him. They wanted to play and be silly with their dad and couldn't understand why he was so exhausted all the time. The Academy was supposed to be a "cool thing" for dad, but it wasn't cool, it was consuming and tiring.

My husband was maxed out from being highly scrutinized for over a 1000 hours of training and his patience wore thin. He was exhausted from memorizing countless codes, observation skills, scenarios, how the media affects police business, hostage negotiations, less lethal weapons, ethics training, racial profiling, use of force and all other things Law Enforcement related.

As the weeks drudged by and the intensity continued, I began to feel effected by it all. I spent much more time alone with the kids then I had imagined I would and I felt less like a side-by-side partner with my husband who was withdrawing in a need-to-pass-Academy shell but felt more like a single parent of three kids trying to work out this thing called life. It was never a matter of my husband not caring, or wanting me in a single-parent feeling role, but the demands of the Academy were higher than we had ever anticipated and finding a balance seemed nearly impossible.

As the saying goes, the last few miles of the race is always the hardest. With only a few weeks left in the Police Academy my husband was operating on burn-out and so was I. While I clung tightly to my faith, I found that my rose colored glasses had a huge crack in them as things were definitely looking different than they had at the beginning of the race.

The weeks wound down and the pressure to succeed was higher than ever. Although my husband tried to act confident and positive on the outside, the mounting stress and concern for seeing the Academy through successfully was marked on his face and even displayed itself through a very unpleasant, odorous night sweat, a.k.a stress sweat. He often put a towel down on his side of the bed to soak up all the wetness. Then came an unexpected infection.

My husband's right eye somehow became very infected right towards the end of the Academy. If it was Pink-eye, he would have to miss at least a week of the Academy due to Pink-eye being highly contagious. If he did have to miss a week, then after everything he had been through, it would mean he would be dismissed from the program. The stress of it all was too much as we both realized we had reached a point of no longer being in control. My husband didn't ask for the eye infection or do anything to purposely get it, it just happened and now it could change everything.

His classmates, while otherwise supportive, freaked out when they saw his red puffy eye. They didn't say it, but my husband new, if it was pinkeye, they didn't want him anywhere near them because it could mean their potential dismissal as well.

My husband had an appointment set with a doctor to find out the status of the infection and while waiting, we discussed the possibility of being dismissed from the program and what that meant. Wanting to maintain my support of his goal to complete the Police Academy, I said what I felt was the right thing to say: *If by chance you are dismissed from the Academy you can start over.*

The idea of starting over was just too much for him to even consider. Not knowing how things would turn out, he did the only thing he knew to do at that point, he surrendered his will of completing the Police Academy to God. It wasn't an easy thing to do but he felt like he had no other choice. He had reached the end of his rope and just surrendered the situation to God, feeling both a sense of defeat and trust that God's will would be done one way or the other.

After a thorough examination, the doctor concluded that my husband had just a regular eye infection possibly brought on by dust particles irritating the eye and that there was no need to be concerned about Pink-eye. Though his classmates were still leery and kept their distance until his eye cleared up, we both were relieved to know that God had kept the door open and soon my husband would cross over from Police Academy Recruit to a Police Officer.

Eight long months later, finally reaching the last paper badge with the plastic blue Officer on it, we were all drained but also overjoyed as we witnessed my husband and the other twenty eight out of the initial sixty-eight recruits who had started the Academy together, sworn in.

"On my honor, I will never betray my badge, my integrity, my character or public trust. I will always have the courage to hold myself and others accountable for our actions. I will always uphold the laws, my community and the agency I serve."

With my rose colored glasses dangling from my face and the hard part behind us, or so I thought, we officially stepped into the first year of blue life.

Again, I had expectations, but not nearly as rosy as I had prior to the Academy. Nonetheless, I did have some expectations of our new blue life and what it would look like for my husband and I along with our three children ages fourteen, nine and three.

One of the expectations I had of myself that first year was to be an excellent listener. I imagined my husband would be sharing we-busted-the-bad-guys stories with me and I planned to exercise excellent listening skills which would not only make me a fantastic wife but would allow me to feel connected with my Officer.

As with most all of his graduating class, my husband

started out working in the jails, overseeing three-hundred plus inmates. I figured his first batch of stories would include inmates being incarcerated for stealing cars, selling drugs or some sort of minor domestic violence but instead, the very first real on-the job story my husband shared with me was one that involved an unimaginable injustice done to a child. As he began to share just a bit of the shocking details, I couldn't handle it. I cut him off, despite the look in his eyes that said he needed to get it off his chest and asked him not share those type of stories with me.

I am an extremely tender-hearted soul but I still thought I could handle what he might tell me. A few details into that first story and I realized, I was wrong.

Listening to some of the heavier details of his job came off the table right from the start and while I felt bad that I wasn't tougher, I wasn't overly concerned because I knew there were a million other little ways I could walk this blue line with my Officer and I was determined to do so especially that first year.

Looking back, I would have to say that as challenging as the Academy was for my husband and our family, it was the first year after the Academy, while actually working the job and living the blue life that was the ultimate rude awakening and extreme reality check for me.

What I noticed about my Officer during that first year was that his suspicions of others were on constant high alert. He had just come out of months of intense police training where day after day trusting no one, suspecting everyone until proven otherwise was drilled into him, so I couldn't exactly blame him. He did try his best to leave that mentality at work but having an overly cautious, intense thinking, need to control his surrounding type of mindset on the job couldn't help but overflow into his personal life outside of work. I on the other hand, am the polar opposite.

I tend have the same mindset as Brenda, one of the beautiful behind the blue wives who shares her story in another chapter which is, lets all believe in unicorns and happy things. I don't mean to say I'm unrealistic or live La-La land but I have been known to have a personality more like an animated cartoon character and I'm bent toward believing the good verses the bad.

Having such opposing natures that first year, really made it hard to relate to one another let alone as wife of an Officer to understand how to walk the blue life with my husband. This would have been a challenge if it had been just my husband and I but throw three children into the mix, one being a teenager trying desperately to find her own identity, it made for an extremely tough first year.

Things like having to celebrate holidays on a different day that perhaps upset other wives weren't really the issue for us because even as a courier for Fed-Ex, my husband often had to work late on Christmas to get the presents delivered on time. Being that he was like Santa for his job, we just planned our family Christmas time around it. However, within that first year there were some things that became very clear to the kids and I; things that became embedded in our thinking over the years. Some of which became clear by what my husband directly said but mostly by what the kids and I picked up on as we observed him working out his new career as a Law Enforcement Officer.

Whether we discussed it or not, what became clear by the end of the first year was this:

1. Not everyone likes police so to be protected, tell no one what dad does.
2. Don't be paranoid but always look over your shoulder.
3. Think ahead in order to be safe.
4. Keep your circle small.

Understanding it now, I can pinpoint this first year in Law Enforcement as the time that I could have really benefited from having blue line sisters. Wives who understood the feeling of seeing their man become hyper-focused on doing an excellent job as an Officer and how in the midst of it all getting caught up in applying the intense training, becoming bent toward protecting everyone to a fault. I would have loved to have read a blog or book or better yet have had a seasoned woman tell me how blue wives can successfully bring their Officers back to a calm place.

But as I've said, there wasn't the same type of resources available then as there are now. Besides, my husband by nature has never been one to socialize with co-workers no matter where he worked, so it was no different once he joined the Police Department. I never met any of his partners or their wives, we never attended any department functions, other than one retirement party for his favorite Judge, thirteen years into his career, so leaning on a few good Law Enforcement sisters in those early, adjusting years, wasn't something I knew I could do.

Ironically, it's through the writing of this book that I even discovered that there are wives of Officers out there ready, willing and able to come together and support one another.

The thing about "not connecting" with other Law Enforcement wives that I didn't even realize until working on this book is that, as an Officer's wife you tend to internalize everything and assume no one else really understands the odd things you experience as a wife behind the blue. Not knowing that I even had the need for other blue sisters and how much it would have helped, I pressed on and blossomed in other areas while keeping our blue line life and all the quirks that come with it, private.

A few years into this private blue life, something happened one summer night that I'll never forget. My husband and I were fast asleep when a loud popping sound went off. In one fluid motion my husband rolled over, scooped me in his arms, off the bed and onto the floor, covering me with his body. I was still half asleep and not sure what was happening. A few seconds later the popping sound went off again and this time there was a bright white flash of light outside our window. It took a few moments of assessing the situation while still covering me before my husband realized it was someone in the neighborhood setting off early fireworks.

Waking up and coming to my complete senses while still underneath my husband, I realized a few things. First, that I was relating less and less to the type of job my husband had in Law Enforcement and to the type of situations he dealt with that would cause him to fly out of the bed and cover me the way he did. Next I realized that because of the job he would never stop being on hyper-alert and I needed to accept that just a little more than I had been. Finally and most importantly, I was reminded of my brave, loving husband who I was proud of as a man, not just as an Officer and who had demonstrated in an instant, Policeman or not, that he would protect me with his life.

Recently our oldest daughter, now 31 years old, mentioned her youthful expectation of when her dad became an Officer. *"I thought it was going to be very cool. I thought dad was going to be like the policemen we saw at school who gave us stickers. But it wasn't like that because I found out Officers really do have to work."* The idea that she was surprised way back when that her dad really had to work as an Officer made me chuckle. She then mentioned something that warmed my heart to its core. She talked about her dads nature to be overly cautious and protective in general and much more so after becoming an Officer and while she didn't always understand his reasonings as a teenager, she admits, *"I never had anything to worry about because I always felt safe with dad."*

As I listened to my daughter share her thoughts, I recalled one wife behind the blue sharing how it was much easier for the family once the children were older and really understood the long hours, the quirks, the intensity and over protectiveness with their dad being an Officer. Oh how I could relate to her story, particularly now that my children, ages thirty-one, twenty-five and eighteen have all come to that same understanding for themselves. As much as you try to explain to little children or even teenagers how their dad is out protecting a community of people from bad guys and how the interaction with so many bad guys can sometimes effect him, all they really care about at that age is wanting daddy home. I can certainly understand that as I'm sure all blue wives can.

I actually did make friends with one Law Enforcement

wife Una, who shares some of her story in a later chapter, a few years into my husbands career. Una and I became friends because our kids were participating in karate together. We didn't realize until our husbands greeted one another at the karate studio that we were both wives of Officers and that our husbands worked for the same department.

Meeting up with Una today for coffee, we talked about the fact that we have known each other a pretty long time now and yet with as many coffee dates and visits she and I have had over the years, we could count on one tiny hand how many conversation actually included talking about our husband's jobs in Law Enforcement or our roles as their wives. The only conversation I recall was one having to do with the possibility of our husband's taking the Sergeants exam. Other than that, we centered our conversations on our faith and on our personal demanding job of raising kids.

Until today, Una and I never talked about what it's like being a wife of an Officer and how it affects the family both good and bad. We never thought to share with each other all these years as to what worked and what didn't during the harder times when our husbands were exhausted from dealing with the ugly of uglies. It wasn't because either one of us were clueless, on the contrary, Una and I, without realizing it had somewhat of the same mindset, of not talking to others about what your husband does.

But today, Una and I spent about an hour and half chatting with each other and for the first time in our entire friendship we talked openly about being a wife behind the blue. In the midst of our conversation, Una happened to mention a book, *Emotional Survival for Law Enforcement: A Guide for Officer and Their Families by Dr. Kevin Gilmartin*. She told me how she and her husband read this book years prior and it helped her husband really understand the need for "being present" with his family, something that is a challenge for Officers whose minds are consumed with the nature of the job.

The moment Una shared this valuable tool, I said to myself, *There! Right there. That is the reason wives behind the blue need to connect openly with each other. So they can share tools with each other that have helped them as blue wives along the way.*

Una mentioning the book struck a cord personally because being truly present has been one of my Officer's greatest challenges and my biggest complaint from almost day one. If I had pushed past the "don't talk about what your husband does" mentality way back when and shared with Una the challenge of being present for my Officer, she could have easily encouraged me by sharing how her Officer was gaining insight on that very subject.

Fortunately, the newer generation of blue wives now have Google at their fingertips to discover these resources but almost 20 years ago, it was a matter of finding a book on the bookshelf of a bookstore at the right time, if you were lucky.

Though my husband is now looking to retire in just a few years, having a real Officer's wife to Officer's wife talk with my trusted friend Una today was encouraging and it confirmed all the more why I'm writing this book.

Now that I am branching out and speaking with other Law Enforcement wives through the writing of this book I have noticed a similar theme of concern. Many wives of Officer's feel that their husband's job is all consuming. The Law Enforcement wheels just seem to be churning 24/7 and

I've heard more than one wife say that every once in awhile she wishes there was an off switch for her Officer.

Again, I completely relate. I felt exactly the same way by the time our middle child hit the teen years. We had already been through one rough patch of teen years with our oldest and by the time "teen-i-tess" hit the second one, I wanted to turn off the 24/7 Law Enforcement switch so I could have my husband's undivided attention so he could fix all the hormonal chaos in the house.

It's not that he wasn't doing a great job as a husband and father because he was, but the 24/7 on-the-job mindset is real and extremely hard to balance at times.

I held so tightly to this feeling of wanting to flip the off switch to all the training, the hyper-focus of the job and every police detail that constantly flooded his brain during this season of raising teenagers that a root of bitterness started to develop inside me.

If you've ever dealt with any bitterness then you know how you don't always see it coming, it just sneaks into your heart and mind and before you know it, feelings of bitterness can become just like the job of Law Enforcement—All consuming.

Little by little I went from having a sense of pride as I believed my husband had a call from God on his life to be an Officer and make a difference in the community he worked in to feeling resentful over the long hours, endless overtime, range practice, tactical training, the endless commuting, and just all of it. I was tired of feeling like a single parent and ultimately began feeling sorry for myself.

Once again, this was a key time that I can look back on and see how a seasoned blue line sister could have put her arm around me and explained that these feelings for a wife of an Officer were normal. That the job of an Officer requires a lot and so does being a wife of an Officer. Oh how I would have treasured having another blue wife who had been there, explain to me that it was perfectly normal to feel bitter, resentful or sorry for myself for a time as long as I didn't stay there for too long.

While I wasn't connected with blue wives, I was thankfully plugged in with women from our church. Though I never particularly spoke with them about the Law Enforcement life, I did speak with them about the challenges of raising kids and they helped me by pointing me back to God and my faith in Him during that season. When I think of it now, how wonderful it was to have their spiritual support, I imagine what a powerful combination it would have been if I had had their support combined with support from my blue sisters.

Since that season of my life, I have spent countless hours chatting it up with God about the bitterness that can easily take root for anyone, let alone a wife of an Officer. How for a season it grabbed a hold of me and how sometimes, even now as we continue to walk the blue life and deal with its many demands, if I'm not careful, a root of bitterness can still pop up. But how grateful I am that God continues to work in me, grow me and shape me into who He has created me to be.

While I would prefer to tell you that I have been the most understanding, completely supportive, easy going, perfect wife behind the blue just as I had assumed I would be at the start, that's simply not true. The truth is I have struggled at times with this high calling of being a wife of an Officer mainly because I haven't always wanted to share my husband with the brotherhood, and the community he protects. I'd prefer to keep him for myself and the kids, free from the hyper-focused, protect at all cost, switch that rarely turns off. But then again, that's the very thing that makes me so proud of my Officer.

Thankfully, when I struggle, when I fall short of my own expectations as a wife behind the blue, God is there patiently reminding me that He has not called me to be a perfect Officer's wife any more than He's called my husband to be a perfect Officer. He has simply called us both to walk out this life and this blue line calling with our heads up, trusting Him.

As women it is our God given nature to nurture and support at all costs those whom we love. We put our kids before our own needs as well as our husbands which isn't necessarily bad when there is balance but what I have come to learn is that without faith and a strong support system of seasoned, like-minded sisters around you who have been there, done that and succeeded, life, especially life as an Officer's wife becomes much more challenging than it needs to be.

One wife behind the blue recently asked me if I felt that my faith grew stronger because of my husband being an Officer. It was an excellent question and one that I have reflected on many times since she asked.

I explained to the this sweet sister that when I discovered that God was really real and not just "the man upstairs." And the moment I understood that He actually wanted a relationship with me, I gave my heart to Him and never turned back. That was years before my husband ever became an Officer and thankfully I have been growing stronger in my relationship with God, one day at a time ever since. So the answer to her question is Yes and No. My faith hasn't grown stronger because my husband is an Officer but choosing to develop a daily walk with God through prayer, reading the Bible, participating in women's Bible studies, and a good church has played a significant part in making me the strong woman of faith that I am today. Had I not been seeking God daily for my own spiritual growth, while at the same time covering my Officer in prayer, I am certain I would not have made it through the bitterness and self pity that so easily entangled me as a Law Enforcement wife.

Today, as I write this chapter, sharing a bit of my story as a wife behind the blue, the best advice I can share with my blue sisters from my own experience is to take off those rose colored glasses if you happen to wear them as I tightly as I did and know that some seasons will be tough but have faith because God has called you to an honorable task. Everyday may not be perfect; somedays you might feel bitter when there is no off switch for your well trained Officer, but fear not. God will guide you and equip you for this high calling as you lean on, trust in and rely on Him.

A Wife's Advice

1. Seek out a circle of sisters that include other wives of Officers, spiritual advisers, along with honest and silly sisters. A variety pack of women in your life will help you more than you can imagine.

2. Start a connection journal. One successful way my husband and I stayed connected through the demands of his job early on was by keeping a journal by the coffee pot. We would write each other little notes of encouragement and love. It helped me a great deal to look through the pages of the journal and be reminded of our connection, during my bitter season.

3. Never stop explaining to your children why dad does what he does. Even though they've heard it before, at different stages, they need the reminder because children can easily mis-understand the Law Enforcement life.

4. Always remember that God has equipped your husband for his calling as an Officer and He has equipped you as a wife behind the blue.

A Wife's Prayer

Dear God,

I pray a blessing upon each and every wife behind the blue. Remind her that you are there for her during the good times and the bad and that she has no need to fear. Encourage her, support and protect her and give her strength to be the wife and woman you've called her to be. Cover her always, never taking your eye off of her, and do the same for her Officer.

My Thoughts:

The police aren't there just to be admired in their uniforms. God also has an interest in keeping order, and he uses them to do it. That's why you must live responsibly—not just to avoid punishment but also because it's the right way to live.

~Romans 13:5

WENDY
A WIFE BEHIND THE BLUE 4 YEARS

When Wendy and her husband started dating he was already in the military which gave Wendy an introduction to the risks that come from a job that involves protecting others. It wasn't long into their dating relationship that Wendy knew that her man had his sights set on becoming a Law Enforcement Officer and felt his military lifestyle prepared her fairly-well for what lie ahead.

As her husband stepped into his new position as a Patrol Officer, Wendy envisioned that people would see him exactly the way she did, as a good man who willingly puts his life on the line daily for the protection and well being of others. In other words, she assumed others would view her husband as a hero.

Reflecting back now, she wonders if what she had originally envisioned was a bit unrealistic or childish, but at the time her sincere impression was that her husband was stepping into a role that people would fully appreciate, just the way she did. His role was to serve and protect the people and therefore she believed her husbands passion would be evident to all through his chosen profession and most importantly his actions on the job.

Wendy also wholeheartedly expected to be able to openly express just how proud she felt of her husband as an Officer and to boldly demonstrate her support of him and of Law Enforcement in general, in every way possible, only that wasn't the case. It wasn't long before Wendy had a rude awakening and began to see that not all of the people her husband worked to protect appreciate his role.

Unfortunately a few bad apples in Law Enforcement in recent years along with the mass reach of social media has caused some of society's negative views about the police to spread like wildfire, Where Wendy once envisioned boasting about her husband's job, she now finds she has to hide the fact that he is a Law Enforcement Officer who wears a badge with desires to protect his community. This reality has been the hardest part for Wendy of being a wife behind the blue.

She had known she would probably have to swallow a lot of her own fears to make room for the baggage her husband would bring home on a day to day basis due to the nature of his job. She felt prepared for the logistics of hard days, long hours, lots of papers, overtime, and even the challenge of listening to tragedies and hard calls her husband would experience but she never expected to have to suppress her pride in her hero or to struggle with the inability to overcome the opinion of others.

She had hoped to have a thicker skin about it all and on some days she admits to doing alright, but on other days, the negative comments on social media, verbal attacks on Law Enforcement in the news or on the lips of people in general seem a bit too much for Wendy to handle. Nevertheless, she makes an effort everyday to work on it.

When asked about the good and bad of being a wife of a Law Enforcement Officer Wendy shares,

"When you are married to a man whose passion is the badge, the brotherhood, the coveted Thin Blue Line, then you are motivated to focus on that truth and not all the ugly. I know my husband cares about his community, loves the work he puts in, and gives it one-hundred percent of his dedication which to me translates into a happy husband. That is the good side.

The bad on the other hand, are a direct result of the job.

Unlike any other job in America, this job creates a target on our men. We are living in a time where police are made to be villains instead of the good guys and we are forced to shy away from standing proud because of this threat. It was an ugly conversation to have with our kids, to explain why we can't tell strangers their daddy is a Police Officer even though they are beaming with pride. The news, the comments on social media, all of it equals this massive pool of negativity to where if you let it, it can drown you. I've gotten sucked in too many times, but I have to stick my head up long enough to remember, my husband's heart is true and what he is doing does not reflect the opinion of others."

Not letting the particular community that voices their dislike of Law Enforcement consume her thoughts or actions keeps Wendy in a place of continually re-adjusting her mindset so that her heart does not become heavy. Without a regular re-adjustment mentally as well as spiritually, Wendy has come to recognize just how easy putting on a hat of resentment or hatred actually is.

Though overcoming the opinions of others is an area of regular struggle for Wendy, seeing how her husband handles his profession with grace and bravery and how he simply lets the negative view of some roll off his back, Wendy is reminded to practice the same and is learning to let the negative go, one day at a time.

Choosing to stay focused on the positive sides to Law Enforcement and her role as a wife of an Officer, Wendy shares a few tried and true tips with other wives behind the blue that have helped her.

A Wife's Advice:

1. Find your strength in something that is consistent. Mine is God. I continually lean on the promises of the Word and know that He is my peace.
2. Don't let the job define your marriage. It's his honorable title, but it's not your marriage title.
3. Continue to date each other, have fun, and make sure you are his soft place to fall.
4. Be honest with your husband when situations come up, don't hold it in. You don't have to be strong all the time, your husband is still your protector too, so don't be afraid to speak what's on your heart.

A Wife's Prayer:

Dear God,

I am so proud of my husband and his job as a Law Enforcement Officer but not everybody feels the same way as I do. Some people have negative views and ugly comments about those working in this profession and at times it grieves me. Help me to not put unnecessary importance on what others may think or say. Keep me from the temptation of wearing a hat of resentment and instead help me to keep my eyes on you and focus on your promises that are right, true and good.

My Thoughts:

Be strong. Take courage. Don't be intimidated. Don't give them a second thought because God, your God, is striding ahead of you. He's right there with you. He won't let you down; he won't leave you.

~Deuteronomy 31:6

ISABEL
A WIFE BEHIND THE BLUE 3 YEARS

Isabel and her husband had been high school sweethearts with a fairy-tale romance that led to marriage at the age of twenty-one. Neither of them had ever discussed or even considered a career in Law Enforcement up to that point. On the contrary, her husband worked in the field of finance for a decade before realizing that his true passion wasn't in credits and balances but in helping people in a more personal sort of way.

At age twenty-nine when her husband told her of his desire to become a Police Officer, Isabel recalls a feeling of *naive excitement* about entering into the unfamiliar territory of Law Enforcement.

With a new found passion in his heart, Isabel's husband made a bold career move and applied for a position as a dispatcher for the police department in his hometown. Although he actually had no experience in that particular field, he did have qualities that allowed him to be a strong candidate for the position. To his delight he was hired and quickly excelled as a dispatcher. In no time, he developed respect and friendships with his co-dispatchers, the Officers, and the employees working in other areas of the department.

While he thoroughly enjoyed his position as a dispatcher, it didn't take long for his desire of helping and serving people to grow beyond that position. Soon enough, his heart was telling him to go out on the streets and join the men in blue. He enrolled in the Police Academy that was held at a nearby community college and attended school during the day while continuing to work full-time in dispatch at night.

For nine months, he worked diligently to pass every test along with every physical training exercise required. Despite his lack of sleep and little time spent at home, Isabel's husband eventually graduated at the top of his class in the uniform he would be wearing on the streets as a sworn Officer with the department that offered him a full-time position upon his graduation.

Isabel recalls graduation day as if it were yesterday.

There I was, having made it through nearly a year of watching him work himself to complete exhaustion, while giving birth to our third child and working full-time myself in the middle of it all. I was proud and ready to take on this new life as a blue line wife. I had read the books I needed to read and joined the social media groups I needed to be a part of to not only gain a group of supporters, but to prepare myself for what was to come. I had a good plan. But then God laughs at your plans.

With no real family background or personal experience in Law Enforcement, Isabel had made some assumptions early on. She pictured her husband's new role as an Officer the way it seemed to be depicted in the books and stories she had read. She assumed her husband would work his shifts coming home on time some days and late others. She assumed he would have the opportunity to help people and that those people would admire him for the selfless job that he had taken on. She really didn't know exactly how things would look, but comfortably assumed throughout his career he would take on different assignments to gain experience, get promoted and continually fulfill his passion of assisting others through his amazing career choice. And she would be joyously by his side every step of the way.

She made plans to be a part of the group of wives within the department and with other departments and looked forward to connecting. She was more than ready to start collecting her Blue Line apparel branded with her own badge of honor; *being the Mrs. to a Mr. Police Officer.* She eagerly anticipated what it would be like waiting for her husband to arrive home after his shift so she could listen to all of the stories he would tell her about his day. Her heart's desire was to be ready to support anything her husband wanted or needed regarding his job and would do so with a sincere smile on her face because she was genuinely proud of everything he was doing. Fast forward three years into her husband's Law Enforcement career and somethings have changed while others have not.

What has definitely not changed is how Isabel still finds herself smitten when seeing her husband in his uniform. She loves to visit him while he is working and watch the positive reactions people have towards him. She consistently feels a major sense of pride when she sees her husband working out his passion.

However, with a few years of living the Law Enforcement life under their belt, what has changed for Isabel is the naive excitement she once had. She has come to an understanding that sometimes life doesn't work exactly as you plan.

Though considering herself a strong women of faith, Isabel

has found herself questioning God's plans about what He is doing in their lives almost daily. She had believed that the books and stories of being the wife of a Law Enforcement Officer had significantly prepared her but discovered a hard truth. Until you live it, you really have no idea.

Initially Isabel predicted that there would be some holidays, family and school functions, and other events that her husband might have to miss due to the nature of the job. However, she didn't quite predict the intensity of the struggle she and their children have when daddy is not there on Christmas morning or has to work on their birthday or on other important occasions.

The books she had read hadn't fully prepared her for the loneliness she felt or for the affectionately named "single-married parent" life that comes with having children and being a wife of an Officer.

She had understood that there would be long hours but never imagined just how much overtime her husband would *actually* have to work. Whether it is voluntarily overtime, being held over at work because the next shift is short, drowning in paperwork and reports, or having to sit with a trainee while they take hours to finish their work under supervision. All of the necessary long work hours equal more time away from home.

After the first two years of his new career, Isabel and her husband agreed that their children needed constant at home support and so Isabel left her work world to stay home and be a full-time caregiver for her family. Although she values every moment of caring for her husband and children, leaving her work environment created personal challenges. In addition to leaving her work, Isabel and her family moved thirty miles from their hometown, leaving behind family and close friends in order to live in a smaller town with better schools, and reduce the risk of running into someone who may have had negative contact with her Officer. Though the changes were necessary for the family it has created a sense of loneliness and disconnect for Isabel that she didn't expect.

Isabel says she attends a mom's group at church twice a month and stays in contact with friends the best she can, including friends she meets through social media groups but still, she struggles with feeling loneliness at times as she misses her *best friend* and partner.

As a Law Enforcement wife, Isabel believes it's important to stay strong for their four girls but admits that there are days that she feels close to breaking and finds it difficult to reach out to others. Because reaching out can be difficult, she has often considered the problems she faces as her problems alone but is slowly learning that she is not alone. There are other Law Enforcement wives out there who live this life and feel the exact same way. Other women who are learning the balance of supporting their Officer while taking care of themselves and reaching out and connecting with other wives when the struggle gets a little too hard.

Isabel often finds herself contemplating this unique life she now leads and shares her thoughts.

Do people working in "normal" professions fear that someone they may have arrested is going to follow them home one day and cause harm to their family? Not typical of a person with a desk job or a safe career. Luckily, we found an amazing home with neighbors in Law Enforcement which we are becoming good friends with and understand this "odd" life we live. Since my husband is working swing shift I spend many afternoons and evenings alone which is something I never thought I would be doing as a wife. After all, you marry someone so that you can have endless sleepovers and feel safe at night knowing they're right next to you. You do not marry someone because you plan to sleep alone so that other people can sleep safe. It is a life of loneliness that I never thought I would have to endure as a married woman.

Learning to work through her feelings of loneliness, another challenge that has caught Isabel off guard is the lack of support from some elected officials and citizens in the state they are from. Various new laws, regulations and even negative public opinion are now preventing Officers, who risk their lives protecting people from doing their job. Without full support from officials and citizens it is now considered a risk to show your pride and support to the world by wearing a t-shirt with a blue line or placing a Law Enforcement flag on your car. Isabel never once imagined that she would have to hide what her husband does for a career when all she wants to do, even as she adjusts to the challenges she faces as a blue wife, is to shout to the world that her Officer is a superhero and not a villain.

While always a superhero in her eyes, Isabel has noticed some changes in her husband since graduating from the Academy. He is still passionate about serving and helping others but there is a bit of hardness of the heart and mind that has naturally developed because of the job. While her husband is compassionate enough to put on the uniform everyday and give everything he has to his career while risking his life for others, there is also a loss of empathy for certain people and situations because of dealing with the same type of ugly over and over. Many in this profession find it hard to feel bad for the type of person who continually gets arrested for a particular crime but will do nothing to help themselves despite being given multiple opportunities.

It takes a special kind of person to do the job that Officers do, to see the things that they see, and yet still find a way to not bring all the emotional and mental baggage home that comes from their job.

Despite having to look over their shoulder when off-duty because they might run into someone who they have arrested. Despite the need to sit in a specific seat when going out for dinner with family or friends where they can see everyone coming and going just in case there is danger. And despite sometimes being portrayed as a human's biggest enemy which can be stressful and emotionally draining for the spouse, being a Law Enforcement Officer is still an extraordinarily noble job and one that she is exceptionally proud of every-time her husband puts on his uniform.

Isabel loves that her husband is finally doing what he is passionate about even though it is hard, exhausting, and usually thankless. Having been a couple since they were teen-agers, she has watched her husband grow into the amazingly strong, hard-working man he is today.

Isabel no longer has a naive excitement about the Law Enforcement life but instead she now has a realistic under-standing of what it means to be married to an Officer. And as she continues to work through personal areas of challenge, she shares a bit of what she has learned so far with other wives behind the blue.

A Wife's Advice:

1. Get involved in a network of others who live this wonderful, yet extremely hard life. You will need this network of support a lot more than you think.

2. Do not give up on yourself, your spouse, your marriage, family, or life. There are good days, and there will definitely be bad ones where you question your ability. But you will make it through.

3. Be prepared to lose friendships with the people that don't support your spouse's profession or don't understand why your family cannot always make it to gatherings because your schedules do not work with theirs. You will eventually find other friends who do understand.

4. Pray diligently for your Officer's safety and never let him go without a hug and a kiss.

5. Be prepared to smile and nod as he tells you, over and over again, about the things he did at work because that is going to be a major part of their lives. Even if you've heard the same story a dozen times and you did not get the opportunity to tell him about your day yet before he passed out from exhaustion, be there to listen.

6. Learn to shoot because that is going to become the desired activity for date nights and adult time with other Law Enforcement couples.

7. Stay strong but do allow yourself to cry when need be. You are not alone in this. You have the biggest, most supportive family who stands along the blue line with you.

A Wife's Prayer:

Dear God,

You have given my husband a high calling as a Law Enforcement Officer and I love this calling but I had no idea that some days I would feel so lonely, so disconnected and so very disheartened. When I'm feeling this way, remind me I'm not alone. Give me the courage to reach out to others for comfort and support and fill me up with your love, hope and grace every day so that I may have the ability to pour out the same for the Officer you've give me—my husband.

My Thoughts:

Blessed be God, my mountain, who trains me to fight fair and well. He's the bedrock on which I stand, the castle in which I live, my rescuing knight.

~Psalm 144:1-2

Victoria
A WIFE BEHIND THE BLUE OVER 30 YEARS

Victoria's husband was a Police Officer for three different counties during his thirty-five year career in Law Enforcement.

When they met Victoria's husband had already been on the force for two years and was pursuing his job with passion. Victoria worked for the same division as a Records Clerk, Dispatcher and a Reserve Officer which helped her right from the start to have a solid understanding of the life of an Officer. This first hand knowledge made the transition from girlfriend to becoming a wife behind the blue much smoother for her than perhaps other women without the same understanding.

Victoria took note early on that her husband liked to be the best at whatever he did. Initially working in Traffic Accident Investigations he was meticulous about his reports and paperwork. She didn't mind all the extra time the paperwork took because she admired how her husband gave one hundred percent at all times to the job he loved so very much. According to Victoria, her Officer was a perfectionist in the best sort of way, the kind of man who crossed the "T's" and dotted the "I's" to make sure he was giving his personal best. For the first part of his career her husband was all about being the strong, tough cop who enforced the law, made arrests and gave out tickets wherever needed. But overtime he mellowed in his style. Particularly when he began working in Drug Abuse Resistance Education (D.A.R.E.) which is an education program that looks to prevent the use of drugs, gang membership and violent behavior.

Victoria felt nothing but pride as her husband embraced this new position because she knew right off that it was more than just a job for him. He didn't have that just getter-done mentality that often comes from working in Law Enforcement over a period of time. Instead, he had a genuine compassion for the kids in the program and had many conversations with them about where they were headed in adulthood. He loved them, wanted better for them and expected a lot out them. Working in D.A.R.E, he spent many years investing himself into educating young people, showing them they could make better choices. It was rewarding work for him and just one more reason Victoria loved her Officer.

After his extensive work in D.A.R.E, Victoria's husband spent the last three years of his Law Enforcement career serving and protecting a smaller community and as with every other position he held in Law Enforcement, he loved it.

He was one of the oldest Officers in that particular unit but one would never know, as his passion for the job continually caused him to run circles around the younger guys. Victoria recalls with admiration how her Officer would pull up on a scene, take control of a large suspect and handcuff him with ease, seemingly one step ahead of his younger partners.

Due to Victoria working in the same field as her husband

and having been around Law Enforcement in some manner for most of her life made the typical struggles for wives of Officers, such as long work hours, missing holidays and so forth, not much of a concern for her. It also helped that she and her husband found unique ways to work around the craziness of an Officer's lifestyle right from the start.

"We would usually skip the weekends and instead take a Tuesday, Wednesday or Thursday off. Not many wives would tolerate that but because that's the nature of the job, that's just what we did and we got used to it. We both worked holidays and would just celebrate on another day. It was never any big deal. We both worked nights for many years but once we had kids one would work days and the other nights. That's just what we did. We were never normal so it never felt like a sacrifice on my part."

Although Victoria had a solid understanding of the blue life and she and her husband were usually successful at striking a good balance, there were some familiar "wife of an Officer" challenges she had to work through. There were those days when her husband dealt with a little too much ugly on the job, naturally creating stress, and he would come home with a grumpy or snappy attitude. On those days, Victoria and their kids tried to remember it wasn't personal but some days it was a challenge for them all.

Despite her exceptional understanding, there were also times when Victoria felt that her husband's job came before her. As a perfectionist her husband would always want to participate in training to better himself to gain more knowledge and skills for whatever he was presently working on or for whatever area of growth he was looking towards. Wanting to better himself was a good quality but at times it seemed too much.

Reflecting back on the years as a Law Enforcement wife, Victoria believes that she became more sensitive to certain challenges once the couple had children and she was no longer working for the Police Department. Her role had changed drastically once her children were born and while she considered her man an excellent husband and father, he seemed to have "blue blood" so to speak, making his primary role that of a gung-ho Officer, wholeheartedly dedicated to his job.

Though his gung-ho Officer mindset presented occasional challenges for her, more than not, Victoria really understood the passion he had for his job as an Officer and felt blessed to be his wife.

With over three decades of blue line wife experience, Victoria shares some her advice with other wives behind the blue.

A Wife's Advice:

1. Keep your herself strong by having a life outside of your time together with your husband. Take time with your girlfriends or try a sport. That way when he says that he is working overtime you can have dinner with a friend or another mom and her kids. If you don't have interests for yourself you could dwell on him not being around but if you have your own interests it's easier to switch gears and do something else when need be.

2. Don't worry so much about your husband. Worrying doesn't add a minute to his life or yours. Enjoy the time you have together. Ask him about his day and what happened. Remember he needs someone to talk too.

3. Keep your family strong by involving dad when he is at home in the things that involve the kids, the caring of the home and you, his wife. Even the little things like asking for his help in the kitchen will allow him to feel involved and give you both some much needed time interacting with each other.

A Wife's Prayer:

D_{ear} God,

Being a wife of an Officer takes more than just pride in his position, which I have plenty of, but it also takes a great deal of understanding. Somedays I understand all the challenges that come with his demanding job but other days I don't. To be honest, somedays I'm so consumed with my own needs that I just don't feel like being understanding of his. In those moments I need to remember that your love is unconditional and you never stop taking the time to understand. On those more challenging days, give me a fresh wind in my spirit so that I can demonstrate even half of the unconditional love and understanding you show me, to my husband.

My Thoughts:

No weapon turned against you shall succeed.
~Isaiah 54:17 (TLB)

EVE

E ve has a unique insight into being a wife behind the blue as she not only worked as a Law Enforcement Officer for a period of time but also married a Police Officer, twice.

Eve's first husband, presently a sergeant, has been in Law Enforcement for a total of twenty-nine years during which sixteen of those years the two were married.

When they first met, Law Enforcement was new to Eve and she wasn't really sure what to expect that is until she decided to pursue a career in Law Enforcement for herself during the first few years of their marriage. Her career as an Officer lasted only three years however, before coming to the realization that she just wasn't cut out for Law Enforcement. Within those three years she discovered quickly that ninety percent of the situations she dealt with as an Officer were all negative and all that negativity was something she just couldn't handle.

Looking into other departments before officially calling it quits, Eve considered working with the juveniles in the system as an option but a closer look caused her to conclude that working with the youth already in the system wasn't

WIVES BEHIND THE BLUE

going to be much better as there was a great deal of negativity in place in that work as well.

Eve's deepest desires were more in line with helping youth in some way that could potentially encourage them to avoid getting in the system to begin with. As she stepped a way from a career in Law Enforcement and sought out other job options, she eventually found her niche teaching high school and to this day believes it was the best career change she could have made.

Recognizing that she was not cut out for a career in Law Enforcement did not stop her one bit from believing in and supporting her husband as a Police Officer. She knew from the start he was cut out for it and was genuinely happy for him as he pursued his respectable career.

The couple made many friends within the department early on and felt a sense of pride in becoming part of the blue family. And as she settled into her career and he did the same, all seemed to be well and going in the right direction those first few years.

But things began to shift after they began having children. Naturally, with a young growing family, Eve longed to have her husband home to be apart of everything going on with the kids and the household. While she understood his position, having worked in it herself, she began to resent all the overtime hours spent at work whether it be mandatory or volunteer. She was finding that much of her time was spent alone, without her husband, which had never been part of her marriage plan.

While she had always known that his job in Law Enforcement was a high priority for him, she had expected a decent measure of balance between work and home, especially after the children came along. But in time, her husband began putting his job first, above her, above the children, above everything. Doing so, Eve noticed that he became the job. There was no off button as he was 24/7 Law Enforcement which eventually created in him a destructive, above the law mentality. The badge he wore and the authority of the position he held brought out an ugly side that she had never anticipated. Although he had always had a natural bend toward being the best of the best, when compiled with a thwarted mentality about his position, Eve admits, *It wasn't always a good thing.*

As his job intensified, he withdrew more and more from family life and instead was consumed with his work and chose to operate from a do-as-I-say-not-as-I-do mindset on the job, at home and in life in general.

The lack of balance, the negative mindsets, not being home, not being involved in family life and ultimately being consumed with his own position of authority, took its toll. Their marriage did not survive and by the time they divorced Eve was left with a bitter heart toward Law Enforcement because of all that it had cost her.

Ending her marriage in such a detrimental way, Eve never imagined in a million years that she would become the wife of a Law Enforcement Officer again. It was the farthest thing from her mind even when her relationship with a long time friend who happened to be an Officer, and who had been married, divorced, had children of his own, began to grow. Having been good friends for many years prior to her divorce allowed her to feel comfortable enough as friends but never expected something more personal to develop between them. Nonetheless, as their friendship grew, Eve began noticing qualities about her friend that she appreciated more than she initially realized and found herself observing him with different eyes. She noticed that despite his many years on the force holding the demanding position of Sergeant who dealt with issues such as loss of Officers, occasional Officers under investigation, let alone the criminal activity on the street, he didn't respond poorly or out of whack, instead, he remained even-keel.

Eve also became aware that her friend didn't put his work first but instead valued his time with his children and others. He was kind and tenderhearted despite the harsh realities that came from his job.

Her previous marriage had left her cautious, shut down and less trusting of people, particularly those working in Law Enforcement, but because this long time friend consistently demonstrated a positive demeanor in the midst of his career choice, she slowly but surely opened her heart to him. In time, the two fell madly in love and were married.

Where at one time Eve had held tight to a terrible viewpoint of those working Law Enforcement due to her past experience, her present experience inspired a very different way of seeing things.

"Working as a Law Enforcement Officer is very demanding and challenging being that an Officer deals with the worst of the worst on a regular basis but when it comes down to it, the nature of a person can make all the difference to how they approach the job. I just didn't realize someone in Law Enforcement could be so good and so nice."

Eve's husband has taught her that while it's not always easy to be civil, not all policemen abuse their authority or the badge. Her husband loves his job and is great at it but his priority is his wife and family. He is mindful of things that keep the family close like taking his vacation time and not seeking out extra overtime just for the sake of money. No matter how good the money is. When he has paperwork instead of staying late at work, he brings it home and completes it at the kitchen table in order to be apart of everything going on with the family. In other words, Eve's Officer has balance and because of that Eve has regained trust and hope in the blue life and marriage.

Having experience with both sides of the spectrum, Eve offers a few suggestions to wives behind the blue.

A Wife's Advice:

1. Be more assertive about having your husband home. Don't fully be about the job. Supporting your Law Enforcement man is good but setting ground rules for balance is best.
2. Whether you are a housewife, a career woman or a little bit of both be sure to have something for yourself that you enjoy.
3. Wherever you are at in this journey, don't focus on worrying, instead focus on faith.

A Wife's Prayer:

Dear God,

It really is the nature of a person that makes the difference in just about everything they do. As my husband goes about doing his daily duties as an Officer, dealing with the worst of the worst at times, I pray that you keep his nature kind, wise, fair and strong. Help him to maintain balance in every area of his life and help me to do the same.

My Thoughts:

Good people celebrate when justice triumphs, but for the workers of evil it's a bad day.

~Proverbs 21:15

SARAH
A WIFE BEHIND THE BLUE 2 YEARS.

The couple will be tying the knot very soon (before this book is even published) and once they do, Sarah will officially step into the honorable role of a wife behind the blue.

But as of today, as a fiancé behind the blue, Sarah and her Officer are off to an excellent start thanks to their strong communicative relationship where any and all expectations, concerns, plans or thoughts are easily verbalized between them.

Sarah's fiancé is fairly new to his blue line career but has already developed a passion for what he does. When Sarah learned that this was the path he had chosen, she wasn't bothered by it one bit. On the contrary, she felt intrigued as she had never dated anyone in Law Enforcement prior.

As their relationship grew serious, dealing with things like long shifts, overtime and not being able to spend as much time with her fiancé wasn't a problem for Sarah as she considers herself lucky to be one of those people who don't mind being alone. Still, there are those times when they don't see each other for consecutive days not only because of his demanding job but because of her job with the school district that also requires long hours and late nights at times.

It is during these days that roll into each other that she finds herself missing him a great deal. Fortunately, that's where the couple's mutual understanding and solid communication about their expectations have really paid off. It has helped them understand what needs to be done in their personal lives and how to best organize that around both of their schedules.

While at the present moment Sarah and her fiancé have pretty similar, manageable shifts that usually work well for them, Sarah does realize that at some point, after they are married, they will have children. When that happens, and her Officer heads back to patrol having various shifts may be a different story. Despite the adjustments she knows they will have to face after they are married, Sarah is confident that they will find their way and settle into a good routine like they always do. Other than the obvious concerns she has for her future husband's safety while he fulfills his daily job properly enforcing the law, Sarah's main challenge at this point is something that many new blue wives who have had little exposure to the Law Enforcement life in general deal with, and that is fully understanding the scope of what their Officer sees on a day-to-day basis. Sarah admits to the fact that because she is detached from the situations he experiences sometimes it's hard to gauge how deeply it really affects him.

"He's very good at letting me know, without too much detail, what happened in his day and how it's affecting him physically, emotionally, and mentally and this does help me to not take anything personally if he seems a bit distracted or frustrated. But while I can empathize as best I can, I will never truly know which can be hard at times."

This is a very real struggle for wives who love their Officers and want to understand where they are coming from while at the same time not getting overwhelmed by the very real, adverse details that come from the type of work that Officers do.

Though it is all still knew, Sarah is on the right track when it comes to supporting her man as well as herself. She has joined a private social group for Law Enforcement wives and husbands and as connected with two Law Enforcement wives whom she visits and talks with regularly. These two women who have been blue line wives for years have already shared a great deal of insight and advice with Sarah, helping her understand the value of surrounding herself with such women who experience similar things.

As Sarah prepares herself to step into the role of a Law Enforcement wife, she shares what she has found valuable up to this point with other wives behind the blue.

A Soon-to-Be Wife's Advice:

1. The biggest tool I have at my disposal to navigate through this world of Law Enforcement Officers is to have my own path that I focus on. Whether it's my job or a hobby, I make sure that the majority of my time is filled with something I'm doing for myself or contributing to our life as a family. This helps our time apart go much quicker, but also helps alleviate the anxiety that comes with loving someone who puts their life on the line each day.

2. I try not to focus on the what-ifs because that's enough to drive you crazy and that's not healthy for the relationship and it doesn't help him in his role either.

3. Get connected with other wives because It's nice to know that someone else as made it through difficult times, or even to hear the accomplishments of other Law Enforcement families.

A Soon-to-Be Wife's Prayer:

Dear God,

The future is bright as I prepare to marry my Officer. As I step into this new role show me how to best fulfill it. Help me to remember how I feel right now, trusting, happy and in love. There will be days when my husband comes home tired, cranky and not at his best because of having to enforce the law with people who very likely do not appreciate it. During those times remind me not to take it personal and instead give me the ability to love him right where he is at. I may not always understand what he goes through but you do and with that I can trust you.

My Thoughts:

Strength! Courage! Don't be timid; don't get discouraged.
God, your God, is with you every step you take.

~Joshua 1:9

A WORD FROM KRISTI NEACE
AUTHOR, SPEAKER AND FOUNDER OF BADGE OF HOPE MINISTRIES

A Reality Better Than Dreams

Growing up, I could never have imagined that I would one day be married to a walking badge in polyester black. No, the silly games I played pointed to my future husband as a banker or a doctor, someone who made a decent living working a "normal" job like everyone else.

I guess I wore those same rose-colored glasses as I imagined and planned out dinners at 5:00 PM each day, holidays with family gatherings, spur-of-the-moment get-a-ways, sleeping blissfully in my lover's arms at night without a care in the world, and a "Better Homes and Gardens" type boudoir with not a stitch out of place.

What I received? I received the polar opposite of my imaginary dreams. I married a Police Officer...a human target for hatred, bias, and revenge and a buffer between good and evil.

I received countless unknown dinner times with food cold on the stove two hours later; holidays and special occasions as a single parent due to last minute shift changes; plans a year in advance only to be yanked because someone fell ill or got hurt on the job. And the boudoir? Ha! I'm doing good when I get the bed made before I go to work, as I never know when he is going to be in it asleep after a long call out in the middle of the night—gun, handcuffs, bullets, notepad, and pocket knife laying haphazard on the nightstand or bathroom sink; a solemn reminder of the danger he faces.

But I also received a man who has a heart the size of Texas, even to the extent that he would hop on a plane and travel to Orlando in the days following a horrific mass shooting, just to comfort his fellow Officers dealing with so much sadness and struggle.

Being the wife of an Officer can be one of the most challenging occupations. Yes, I call it an occupation because it becomes your life. Officers are on call 24/7, whether you want them to be or not, and so are you, their spouse.

As I sit here thinking back over tragic Officer-involved events this year in New York, Ohio, North Carolina, Kansas, Oregon, and so many other states, I am shaken by the thoughts of my "sisters" who have lost their husbands at the hand of a cold-blooded killer. It is the greatest fear of a Law Enforcement spouse. That knock on the door telling you he won't be coming home. Things will never be "normal" again for these special ladies... if we can even call police life by that title—*normal.*

No, this occupation has its risks—great risks, but even so, most spouses of Officers will tell you that it's worth it... every bit of it. There's a certain swell of pride within us that cannot be overshadowed by any negativity or hatred that this world sometimes dishes out. We know who the real men (and women) are behind those badges. We understand the sacrifices they make.

Not a day goes by that our Officers' eyes are not continuously scanning the crowds in movie theaters, concerts, and even at church. Before long, you as the spouse begin doing the same, imagining what action might be taken in case of the "what if?"

In restaurants, the wife of an Officer knows her place. He sits with his back to the wall, eyes facing the door and she in front of him. Some might say his actions seem ridiculous or even cold, yet he will be the first to react if a gunman should enter. For me, I know there is no safer place to be.

The man I married will drop everything at a moment's notice and slip into that uniform and be out the door in a matter of minutes in order to help his fellow brothers and sisters, or someone in need. He doesn't give a second thought to what color or religion, ethnicity or identity, but lives to serve, and does it well.

My Officer has held countless hands of the dying, comforted the grieving, mowed lawns for the elderly, played with children whose drug-addicted mom or dad sat behind cold bars, continued to check in on the mother of a child who accidentally hung herself in her grandparents' front-yard tree, and calmed the fears of a woman seeing demonic beings on the wall behind him.

These are the things the general public doesn't know about my Officer or any of the others out there. They only see what the media wants them to see, not the people—the hearts behind the badge.

Thinking back to my dreams long ago, I see that I sorely short-changed myself. What I conjured up in my mind was a man. What I was given was a hero!

To all police wives out there... you are blessed! Keep fighting the good fight.

For more information on Kristi Neace
or Badge of Hope Ministries visit
www.kristineace.com

"Behind every brave Officer stands a courageous police wife"

BRENDA
A WIFE BEHIND THE BLUE 10 YEARS

B renda had never anticipated her husband saying that he wanted to become a Police Officer. He had been working as an Information Technology (IT) project manager for a number of years and while the job provided well for his family it wasn't really his passion. Because Brenda knew this fact, she often prayed that her husband would eventually find his true passion, only she had no clue that his passion would be in Law Enforcement.

Brenda recalls that it was somewhere between 2006 and 2007 when things came to a head for her husband causing him to make a radical change. For a solid six months he battled with an intense inner struggle. He was unable sleep, his moods were erratic and despite having always been a healthy person, suddenly his health was failing.

Brenda was at a complete loss as to what was going on with her husband during this period of time so she did the only thing she knew to do, she began to pray.

After six long months of praying for her husband while he dealt with an inner turmoil she didn't understand, she received a call from him on a Thursday afternoon that she'll never forget.

"I could tell he had been crying. He said he needed me to come home because he figured it out. I asked him, what do you mean? He said, I've been pushing away from it, I don't want it to be this but God is telling me I need to go into Law Enforcement. Immediately I started crying and asked, what are you talking about? And he said, God told me that I'm going to save somebody's life."

Brenda was in shock and total disbelief at his words. One moment her husband was quietly working behind a desk in IT and now he was saying he was going to become a badge-wearing, gun-toting Police Officer. And on top of that, God had told him he was going to save someone's life.

She couldn't fully wrap her mind around what her husband was saying, yet there was a small part of her that could hear something very real in his voice. After six months of mood swings, sickness and sleeplessness, Brenda could hear a genuine calm, peace and assurance in her husband's voice that hadn't been there for sometime, and she was grateful.

The couple prayed together about this new revelation and as foreign as it may have seemed, they both concluded that it was indeed of God. Upon their conclusion, they gathered their entire family together to fill them in on the news. Brenda's husband explained to family members how at thirty-eight years old, God was leading him to apply to the Police Academy and with that, requested their support as he knew his wife would need extra help with the kids while he pursued this new calling. The entire family responded by praying over the decision and gladly extending their support.

Not long after, Brenda's husband applied for the Police Academy through a local college as well the city's Police Academy, pursuing both simultaneously.

In likeness, Brenda enrolled in a two-week Spousal

Academy which was run by chaplains who desired for women to connect and to help them understand a bit of what their husbands would be going through during the Academy. This particular Spousal Academy offered training at the shooting range along with simulation training which Brenda found to be a tremendous help in relating to some of what her husband would be doing in his new career. To this day Brenda keeps in touch with a couple of the wives who had participated in the Spousal Academy and is better for it.

Another tremendous help early on Brenda says, was an older Christian couple who lived on their street. The husband had been a Detective and immediately upon learning of Brenda's husband's interest in Law Enforcement, the man and his wife took Brenda and her husband under their wing, mentoring them in what to expect on the job and off. With a solid mentoring couple and the full support of her entire praying family, Brenda found herself ready to embrace this new blue life season. As she prayed for guidance over her role, she felt God telling her to be her husbands biggest cheerleader, and not resist the situation but instead support him in every way possible.

And that's exactly what Brenda set out to do. Whether it was making his lunches, bringing his uniform to the laundromat or running a zillion other needed errands, Brenda set her mind on being her husband's biggest cheerleader and focused on making their home safe and comfortable for him.

One of the many ways Brenda chose to support her husband during his time in the Academy was to run with him every day. Not only did he appreciate his wife support in this way but it also benefited Brenda physically as she lost 70 pounds. Before long the couple were in fantastic shape causing their children who observed them to feel extremely proud and excited to be apart of it all.

Upon entering his blue line career, Brenda was completely taken aback by the change in communication between them. Typically a man of few words, Brenda had assumed entering Law Enforcement might cause their communication to suffer but much to her surprise, with her husband finding his passion as an Officer, it created in him a willingness to communicate and share in a greater way than he ever had before.

"I was really fearful that my husband would shut down as opposed to start sharing but what I've notice is that he wants to share, sometimes more than I want to hear. He has to filter some of that for me because I don't like to internalize all of it but his willingness to share has really helped with our relationship."

In the midst of cheering her husband on and the blossoming communication, there were naturally things she had to adjust to. A big adjustment from the start was Brenda's long-time mindset of no guns, swords or weapons in the house.

Coming from a child development background, she held strongly to that mindset as it seemed an obvious danger. Overtime however, she has learned that a big part of supporting her husband is learning how to adjust her own views. They worked through the concerns of properly storing weapons in the house, as well as Brenda's need to know when her husband was armed or not when they were in public. These were things that were new and uncomfortable for her but little by little she adjusted.

About six months into his training, Brenda noticed a few changes in her husbands mindset, one being was the new rule her husband set of not allowing the kids to walk to the mailbox by themselves anymore. Although the mailbox was right down the street and the kids had been walking to it for years, he was no longer comfortable with it. The same was true for going out to different places. Even if they had gone there before, Brenda's husband was no longer comfortable with some of the places they went because he didn't consider them as safe as he might have at one time. As Brenda has come to understand as a blue wife, this is a natural byproduct of extensive police training.

Another byproduct that Brenda has observed is the inability for her husband to shut down. Brenda doesn't necessarily believe it's a bad thing, such as when their daughter went off to college and her husband made a point to meet with the schools security team to discuss their plans in case of active shooters and other emergencies. It's just that every now and again Brenda admits that she would like if there was an off button to all of her husband's superb police training.

As with many wives whose husbands are going through the Police Academy, Brenda recalls one particularly trying night for her husband when he had a great deal of report writing to do. He was feeling the pressure to get it right, especially after being told to 'either get it right or don't come back.' It was 4am when Brenda walked into the kitchen and saw her husband sitting at the table, overwhelmed to the point of tears. His face showed signs of sheer exhaustion so Brenda told him to go lie down for a bit. With only two hours left before needing to return to the Academy, her emotionally, physically and mentally spent husband voiced in defeat that he was unable to go to bed. It was a potential breaking point for him, a crumbling moment that most recruits going through the Academy experience.

Seeing her man so disheartened and not knowing how to help him she walked back into her bedroom and once again did the only thing she was certain could make a difference—she prayed. She asked God to give her husband the strength to finish the reports correctly without any mistakes, allowing it be successful and creating a window of sleep time for her exhausted husband.

Almost a decade later working in patrol, as a Field Training Officer (FTO) and is currently training to become an Emergency Vehicle Operator Course (EVOC) Instructor, Brenda's prayers were clearly answered. Her husband has never forgotten his wife's encouragement and loving prayers from that night.

Today Brenda's husband feels just as passionate about being an Officer as he did in the beginning when God first impressed upon his heart that he would save someone's life one day. Having his wife as his biggest cheerleader has fueled that passion. Yet and still, there have been a few harsh awakenings in his career.

One of them happened about a year ago when he found himself in a situation where he was the only Officer on scene and had to draw his gun on a young man who looked to be only in his twenties. He was unsure if the young man was mentally ill or on drugs but with gun pulled, he had to decide very quickly within himself if he was going to shoot the man if need be. Fortunately, the young man surrendered nulling the need for Brenda's husband to pull the trigger.

Later, when he arrived at home Brenda noticed right away that something was wrong with her Officer as he was closed off and didn't saying anything to her. Brenda gave him his space but a day or two later finally told him, that she could see something was going on and reminded him that she was there when he was ready to talk about it. It was then that he proceeded to tell Brenda about the situation with the young man and how it felt like a defining moment for him to realize that he may actually have to take a life, instead of just saving one. Certainly he knew it was potentially part of his job but that moment made it so real. Brenda and her husband both were grateful that on that night, in that moment, the man surrendered and his young life was spared.

Knowing many of the "not-so-good" things that her husband deals with has not changed Brenda's personal view on the world. She still tends to believe that most everyone is good and describes herself as more of a rainbows and unicorns type of person. Her husband on the other-hand, is not interested in unicorns and due to the nature of his job tends to overlook rainbows and instead zero's in on the not-so-good. With this particular difference between them, Brenda considers it to be a positive burden as she makes a point of helping her Officer see light in the midst of darkness. It may not always be easy for her but just as her husband feels called and is passionate about his a career in Law Enforcement, Brenda feels called and is passionate about being a wife behind the blue.

Having good communication, a very supportive family and a strong foundation in faith has made it much easier for Brenda to work through the natural challenges of being a wife of a Law Enforcement Officer. However, she realizes it's not always that way for every wife and offers some advice from her experience for other wives behind the blue.

A Wife's Advice:

1. New wives need to prepare for the fact that their husbands mindset will change some. It has to in order for them to best be prepared on the job.
2. Be ready to talk when he is. Let him know that you're there but wait until he is ready.
3. Provide opportunities for your husband to rest away from home. My husband always feels like he's got to protect the home so getting away is good. A wife may have to organize it all but it will help him enjoy himself and the rest of the family.
4. As women we tend to become sacrificial and feel as if our things aren't as important but they are. One successful tool we learned is to have interest in each others day. We have a Google calendar and everything is on it. We all have access to it and that helps my husband a lot. He looks at the calendar, sees what I have to do and remembers to ask me about it. Otherwise he would just not have the mindset to think about my day because Law Enforcement can be all consuming. For me, using the Google Calendar makes a big difference because he remembers that my day and the kids day, while different than his, are just as important.

A Wife's Prayer

Dear God,

Help me to always be my husband's biggest cheerleader. Supporting him, encouraging him and lifting him up by my words and my actions. Not just at the start of something new and exciting that he is involved in but on those days on those long, drawn out days when the routine of it all has become overwhelming. On those days when I'm tired of cheering him on, when I feel there is no cheering left in me, remind me that out of all the women in the world, you've chosen me to be my husband's wife and that's worth cheering about.

My Thoughts:

I've told you these things for a purpose: that my joy might be your joy, and your joy wholly mature. This is my command: Love one another the way I loved you.

~John 15:13

EMILY
A WIFE BEHIND THE BLUE 10 YEARS.

Before Emily's Husband became a Correctional Officer and then Facilities Foreman for the Federal Bureau of Prisons, he worked as a contractor building beautiful custom stairs. It wasn't until the building industry began to take a nose dive that her husband even considered the possibility of any type of career change.

According to Emily, going into Law Enforcement actually began as a joke between the two of them. For some reason the couple kept seeing advertisements about a career in Law Enforcement, so much so that they eventually began to take the idea seriously. After a lot of thought and prayer, Emily's husband began applying to several agencies before finally settling on one. Emily had always respected Law Enforcement and thought it to be an exemplary career so when she learned of his decision to pursue it, she was thrilled. Besides, as Emily tells it, the thought of seeing her husband in uniform was something she couldn't resist.

Though there were some natural concerns of the unknown, once the doors opened, Emily and her husband felt confident that God would work out all the details. And that He did.

Emily's husband took to his new career with ease and recalls how he advanced in his position right away.

"In the beginning of his career, for me, the good experiences were the many times he was promoted, particularly within his first 18 months. He has continued to promote even more over the years. Being honored on many occasions with awards for his work. I was and still am very proud of his passion and his drive to always be working towards bettering himself and others."

Taking pride in her husband's work ethics, is only part of the joy she feels as a wife behind the blue. Another joy has been listening to the stories her husband shares with her. Stories of various inmates that he dealt with on a regular basis and having the opportunity to counsel or mentor them. Even if it was only for a brief time her husband embraced the chance to instill some positive light and hope into the inmates lives. These special, unexpected stories are ones Emily knows she will cherish forever.

Along with embracing the good Law Enforcement experiences, Emily has also had to learn how to embrace the bad. Initially the changing schedule every quarter seemed hard and took some adjusting to, but that was nothing compared to her husband having a fellow Officer murdered just 4 months after he started working at the prison.

"We dealt with grief, anxiety, anger, and doubt. Wondering if this really was the career God want him to have."

Losing a brother in blue so early on not only created doubts and fears, but set the tone for an unintentional numbness and desensitization due to the ugly part of humanity.

If that weren't enough, the rough, physical nature of the job, has left Emily's husband with a broken nose, back problems, knee issues, and other injuries received in the line of duty. Yet, in spite of the many collateral damages, Emily's Officer still believes in the goodness of humanity overall, which is why he continues to strap on his boots and his vest day after day.

The disheartening challenges her husband regularly faces on the job has left Emily struggling at times with knowing exactly to help him deal with his doubts and insecurities when they come up. When it all becomes too overwhelming for them, the couple try and step back a bit and remember the time when they first prayed for God's direction. Reflecting on how every door opened and every sign pointed to the direction of Law Enforcement, they find their assurance again. It's then that they are reminded of the many good things that have come from her husband working as a Law Enforcement Officer. They are reminded in those moments of the many inmates counseled and mentored, who may not have been if her husband had not chosen to step through the open blue line door.

Over the past decade, Emily has learned to listen and not brush off any of her husbands concerns. Though she has many other things on her own plate as a women, wife and mother, she makes it a high priority to treat her husband's concerns seriously and give them validity. In the harder moments which often have "gory details" Emily has come to understand the importance of encouraging and uplifting her Officer instead of sinking to the bottom with him.

While the couple typically do not share the ugly details of the job with their children, Emily and her husband do their best at being open and honest with their kids about what is going on with dad at work. Whether it be that he has to stay for another late shift or is coming home with pepper spray all over him and needs some space, the children have come to have a healthy opinion about their fathers vocation and for that, the couple is extremely thankful.

Through the good and bad, Emily has discovered a valuable tool. When she keeps her composure and avoids being reactive to the many things that come from being a wife of an Officer, it helps bring calm to herself and to her family.

In that vain, Emily shares some advice for other wives behind the blue.

A Wife's Advice:

1. Realize that you cannot do this alone. You need God.
2. Your husband can't always be your strength. You will often have to be his. Be his relief. Even if it's sitting in silence together, it helps tremendously. Yes, he needs to be there for you as well, but throwing up every horrible thing that happened to you when he walks in the door is not helpful. Besides, nine out of ten times what he went through that day was probably worse.
3. Don't allow yourself to wallow in self pity. If your husband is on duty at times when you wish he wasn't, take that time to do something for yourself. Blaming him or having a pity party is not going to make the time any easier. It just builds resentment.
4. Be conscious of how you talk about your husbands job around your children. Being honest with them is helpful, but of course be age appropriate with details.
5. When Dad has to miss a family outing or holiday, don't let it spoil the day. Remind your children of the amazing work your husband does. And celebrate those special occasions on his days off. Who cares if it may be a Tuesday night a week later. Your children feed off of your attitude.
6. Keep in mind that the things he sees, hears, and even smells on a daily basis affects him more than you realize. Despite his desire to forget these things, he can't and probably never will so be patient with him.

A Wife's Prayer

Dear God,

Protect my husband's heart and mind from all the negative he sees on a daily basis. Help him process those things instead of internalizing it. Remind him that there are many beautiful things in this world. And that at its core there is still a great deal of good in humanity. Help me to remain calm and composed. When I'm anxious give me the ability to sit still before you so I can come along side my husband and support him when he needs it most.

My Thoughts:

I picked you to live on God's terms and no longer on the world's terms.

~John 15:18

HANNAH
A WIFE BEHIND THE BLUE 19 YEARS

Hanna didn't think much one way or the other about what a job in Law Enforcement might entail. In fact, in her younger, less experienced years, she wasn't necessarily fond of Police Officers. There was no specific reason as to why she felt that way other than believing a bit of the negative stigma associated with Law Enforcement.

Things changed however, after meeting her husband, and particularly after she went on her first ride along with him in 2011.

Sitting as a passenger in his patrol car, observing the routine of starting the engine and calling into dispatch that he was in service and ready for duty, followed by a plethora of issues that he deals with in his work day really opened her eyes and stirred within her heart a greater amount of respect for her husband and his job as an Officer.

Other ride-alongs allowed her to see a side of her husband, at work, that surprised her. Knowing he handled many scenarios throughout his day, she assumed that he would be in pure authority mode at all times but discovered he wasn't always like that. There were certain situations where he could calm down the authority part of his role and be sweet to people. This was something she never expected to see and appreciated this side of his job as much as the other side.

Initially, Hannah didn't think that the sweet or sour aspects of the job would affect her husband or them as a couple much but as time went on and he settled into his career, she knew she was wrong. Working as a Deputy Sheriff and Field Training Officer, dealing with both the good and bad of people, situations and circumstances on a daily basis couldn't help but affect them in some manner. Whether reflecting on stressful stories and events of the day or laughing like crazy about some ridiculous calls that came in, all of it has had an impact on the couple.

One particular challenge for Hannah's husband is his inability to trust anyone anymore. Because he is lied to more than not while on the job, when he's off the clock, he has a hard time shifting gears and believing what "regular" people say. Being that Officers by nature of the job are under constant stress, some days Hannah says her husband is simply burnt out by it all and has a short fuse, making it harder for him to be in a good mood or enjoy the day.

Fortunately, Hannah is typically an understanding person and has developed a mindset of just taking things day-by-day. She believers her role as an Officer's wife is to be strong, supportive and willing to do whatever she can to ensure her husband's mental state of mind remains strong and at peace.

This day-by-day mindset along with having blue line brothers and sisters she can connect with has allowed Hannah to see more good then bad as a wife behind the blue.

Hannah admits it is hard at times to see her husband come home from work upset, tired or injured, as he presently is with a broken back. It makes her feel helpless, but in those moments she tries to maintain her day-by-day mindset and stay positive for her Officer. It is usually during those times that Hannah's husband assures her of something most likely every Law Enforcement husband feels— just having his wife be understanding is what helps him most of all.

Learning to appreciate all that comes with Law Enforcement Hannah shares some advice with other wives behind the blue.

A Wife's Advice:

1. Be the kind of woman who is good at putting yourself in other people's shoes [particularly your husbands]. If you're not naturally that way, it will take practice but it's worth it. This will help you be understanding and more open minded and he'll appreciate it.
2. Some days you simply have to allow him and his needs to come before your own. Don't nag him, learn to bite your tongue especially if he's had a rough day at work.
3. Go on a few ride-alongs. I personally feel that is the best way to truly understand what he does and what he goes through. It helped our marriage and our family and it very well could help yours.

A Wife's Prayer

Dear God,

I would like to be the kind of wife that is understanding and doesn't mind putting her husband's needs before her own once in a while but sometimes that's just hard for me to do. If I'm honest, I would prefer that my husband puts my needs before his and understands me first but I know it doesn't always work like that. Give me the ability to put myself in his shoes and have a willing spirit to meet his needs without demanding he meets mine first because deep down I know that when we give love freely, love freely is returned. Thank you for blessing our marriage day-by-day.

My Thoughts:

The wicked are edgy with guilt, ready to run off even when no one's after them; Honest people are relaxed and confident, bold as lions.

~Proverbs 28:1

IRENE
A WIFE BEHIND THE BLUE 4 YEARS

Having no real exposure to Law Enforcement growing up, when Irene's husband first told her of his interest in becoming a Police Officer, her only real concern was that it was something he truly desired to do for a career and not just something that sounded good for a steady paycheck.

As he assured her that his motives went far beyond a paycheck when it came to the possibility of working in Law Enforcement, Irene felt an ease about it and was completely on board. The more thought she put into it, she realized that her husbands hands on, hard working nature along with his awareness that what he says or does has the potential to change someone's life course and just being the type of man who knows how to balance firmness and grace when necessary, would not only make a good Officer but one that could very well be the "face" of the department in time.

From the start of his career Irene could see that his job had its own set of challenges and so she wanted to make sure that when her husband walked through the door of their home each night he could relax and feel that his home was his sanctuary.

Irene worked hard to create that type of environment, understanding the value of it, but she didn't always find it the easiest thing to do especially during times of loneliness or fear. During those times she focused more on wanting her husband to help out around the house on his day off or even during the few short hours they had before he left for his shift and she longed for him to acknowledge all she did around the house to keep their life going. It wasn't a bad or unreasonable desire but when propelled by Irene's loneliness or fear, it came across in a negative way, creating anything but a peaceful environment.

Looking back, Irene now knows that despite knowing the basics of the job and the challenges they might face, she and her husband really didn't know how to make this new life of theirs work, so they just took it in stride and did their best.

Irene discovered fairly quickly that being a police wife requires a lot of sacrifice and flexibility. Dinners alone, holidays without your spouse, and little time together depending on schedules, were all part of it and she had to find ways to be okay with it.

Learning to be "okay" within themselves and their new roles along with a solid, growing communication has helped the couple a great deal. Together they make it a point to ask specific questions when one of them isn't sure how to handle something. They also work at serving one another and being a little more selfless with each other, which has only enhanced their marriage.

Practicing good communication has been a huge plus and has even allowed the couple to discuss the heavier issue of how arresting criminals, sighting law breakers, trying to maintain peace in hostile environments among many other unpleasant duties that come with the job can sometimes cause an Officer to become jaded if not careful. Talking through this reality helped the couple come to an agreement and clear understanding early on. If his love of serving and protecting others ever begin to show signs of becoming jaded, he would rather walk away from Law Enforcement than stay in it and become bitter.

Four years into the blue life, Irene has learned how and when to give her Officer, now working in the Street Crime Unit, some space with the understanding that he is not always interested in talking about every work related detail. In those times when he is exhausted and needs to shut down, she has learned not to pry and to be okay with it. At other times when he has needed to talk and just one work story alone takes him 30 minutes to share, she has learned to listen and enjoy the time spent with him.

Part of effectively "doing life" as a member of the blue line family for Irene has been understanding that Social media can be poisonous if you allow yourself to be immersed in every post, tweet, or article written about Law Enforcement. With so many misconceptions about Officers and their duties thrown out for the world to see, Irene admits that it can be hard to not jump into a discussion online and take the defensive side.

Much of the time, Irene finds herself pushing through her defensive urges by smiling, nodding, and moving on. However, that practice becomes a little harder to implement when she and her husband are visiting family members who do not understand what he does as an Officer, taking most of their information from the news. In that case, it becomes much more personal with family. However, Irene and her husband have opted for being honest and up front in their discussions with family members instead of defensive and if that doesn't work, Irene admits, they go for changing the subject.

Out of the many different things that vie for her attention as a wife behind the blue, Irene believes the greatest one is making sure that their friendship and marriage is continually thriving. And now with their first child on the way, a thriving relationship is even more important.

"We have learned that our marriage will not thrive if we are not true friends. We've always gotten along really well, but sometimes you can get caught up in discussing work, or errands and tasks that need to be done. We have learned to carve time out during the week for us to do something outside the house, where we don't discuss work or home. This has made all the difference in making sure we still know each other and don't become "roommates." Date nights are key. As of now, we are making baby shopping more like a date where we go grab lunch afterward but other times it's just putting on a movie and scooping bowls of ice cream while leaving work and home discussion behind."

In the midst of working on a thriving marriage, Irene has noticed a few small changes in her husband since starting his work on the force. As a naturally outgoing, goofball type of man who according to Irene, can steal the attention of a room within seconds without being cocky, she has noticed that he has become much more reserved than he once was. He hasn't lost his fun personality, but his keen observation skills and the need to sit at specific tables or booths when they go out in order to scan the room for safety reasons has added to his now reserved demeanor.

The biggest change Irene has noticed in herself is having become less dependent on her husband to entertain her.

Working only part-time, she used to sit around the house and do nothing until her husband came home. Always waiting for him caused her to become very needy like an excited puppy wanting to go out and do things the moment he got home despite his need to unwind and relax from his demanding job. She eventually realized this approach of hers wasn't healthy for either one of them. There had to be balance and so she has learned to do things that she enjoys such as reading, journaling, photography and even starting her own blog which are all creative outlets that she now loves.

Embracing her new independence, supporting her husband's Law Enforcement career while at the same time committed to building a thriving friendship and marriage with him, Irene shares her insight with other wives behind the blue.

A Wife's Advice

1. Understand that fear based living is not a way to live. Get to know yourself better with the time you have alone.

2. Cultivate other relationships that are important to you by investing time into them. Grab coffee, lunch, shop, or go for a walk with a friend when your husband is working long hours. Don't just fill time for the sake of it. Fill your time with worthwhile things and if you don't know what those things are, it's time to learn.

3. Don't be afraid to let your husband know when you need some quality time with him. If you are feeling an overwhelming sense of worry or loneliness, tell him. But also constantly tell him that you are proud of him, and that his hard work does not go unnoticed – better yet, show him that you appreciate him. When you do, it will be reciprocated.

4. Date nights keep the spark alive and the communication lines open. Go out to dinner, see a movie, have a picnic. Whatever it is just make sure you put your phones away, talk to each other and most of all have fun.

5. Marriage should transform us into selfless people. His needs go above mine. This won't ever be perfect, and we will mess up but that doesn't mean we ever stop trying to be selfless with each other.

A Wife's Prayer:

Dear God,

I love that I can depend on my husband but I'm learning that I also need to be independent as well. While I take care of my husband's needs and support him wholeheartedly, I need to learn what I like and discover what I'm good at so we can have better balance together. Focusing on discovering my own interests is scary and exciting but with your help I can understand more about myself which will be even better for our marriage.

My Thoughts:

You're here to defend the defenseless, to make sure that underdogs get a fair break; Your job is to stand up for the powerless, and prosecute all those who exploit them.

~Psalms 82:4

NATALIE
A WIFE BEHIND THE BLUE 16 YEARS

Natalie met her husband years ago when he was in the Academy and she was a Cadet in the same department. Because of her interest in a blue line career, she wasn't shocked or surprised by her husband's career choice and budding Law Enforcement lifestyle.

However, things changed on Natalie's end in regards to working as an Officer when they started a family a little earlier than expected. Although her personal career plans shifted, having her own experiences and desire for a career in Law Enforcement helped her transition smoothly into her role as a wife behind the blue.

A big positive for Natalie when it comes to things associated with the blue life has been picking out vacation time a year in advance and occasionally even having the opportunity to join her husband in picking out his shift choice which depending on his position has been a great consolation for all the time taken away from the home life.

Another positive Natalie says is the *"hyper-aware spidey-senses you gain from being around someone who is hyper-aware all the time."* Gaining spidey-senses through her Officer has allowed Natalie to feel safer and know what to do in bad situations, which is a good thing.

When it comes to the negatives, as with most Law Enforcement wives, all the missed holidays and parties were initially a big disappointment for Natalie but in time she got used to it, concluding that holidays are just a date on the calendar and that there is nothing that can't be rescheduled.

Juggling the schedule of her two active kids without her husband's help because he often has a hard time saying no to extra work however, is more challenging. The couple's children ages ten and twelve play competitive sports with one child having practice in one location and the other child having practice a good fifty miles away. Everything runs fairly well with getting the kids where they need to be when Natalie's husband is there to help, but as every blue wife knows, having her husband get off the clock on time doesn't always happen.

Despite good intentions because of the mandatory overtime and her husbands struggle to say no when it's not mandatory more times than she would like, Natalie will get a phone call five minutes after her husband is supposed to be logged off for the day, letting her know he's not going to make it. In those times when her husband is unable to share the responsibility of taking their kids to practice, Natalie is forced to choose which child can go to practice that day and which one cannot. Each time having to explain to them that one child isn't more important than the other.

As frustrating as that situation can be at times, there is an even bigger issue for Natalie and her family. Currently working as a Sergeant in charge of the Special Investigations Unit along with S.W.A.T Team Leader and Honor

Guard Commander, Natalie shares how she and her family have been followed, chipped at and threatened when grocery shopping, eating out with their kids, and getting gas in their car. One would hope that an Officer whose sole purpose is to serve and protect the community along with his family would not have to experience such things but it does happen. Fortunately, Natalie has found a positive take-away from having to deal with these types of situations. *"It sucks but you do learn how to pick the dirt bag out of the crowd and be more situationally aware."*

Natalie recently asked her husband a question that might do well for all blue wives to ask of their husbands if they haven't already. She asked him what he wishes she understood better about his role in Law Enforcement. His words were kind and sweet, bringing her to the brink of tears as she was reminded why he is such a wonderful husband in addition to being a wonderful Officer.

"All the extra work and hold overs does not mean the job is more important than you. Work isn't the priority, emotionally. It's the means to provide for my family. I still come home to you. This is my home. That is still just my job. I don't love it more than I love you."

Taking the good with the bad from the Law Enforcement lifestyle, Natalie shares her thoughts with other wives behind the blue:

A Wife's Advice

1. Surround yourself with Law Enforcement wives and non-Law Enforcement wives alike. Some will 'get it' and help keep you in check, and others will be a shoulder to cry on.
2. Do things for yourself. I do cross-fit. When I am happy with myself, when I feel my best, I'm a better wife.
3. Understand that life isn't fair. The job isn't fair. So you're just going to have to suck it up and make the best of it. Embrace it. Let the world of Law Enforcement seep into every aspect of your family, so that even your kids are proud.

A Wife's Prayer:

Dear God,

Sometimes life isn't fair. Sometimes the job my Officer does and how it affects our family isn't fair. And I'll be honest, somedays, having to suck it up and embrace where we are at doesn't feel fair either. But the Bible teaches that you God are fair, just, holy and good. In my time of need, especially when the sacrifices we make at home as a family seem unfair, remind me to shift my focus to the truth of your fairness, your justice and your goodness always.

My Thoughts:

God doesn't come and go. God lasts. He's Creator of all you can see or imagine. He doesn't get tired out, doesn't pause to catch his breath. And he knows everything, inside and out. He energizes those who get tired.

~Isaiah 40:29

DANA
A WIFE BEHIND THE BLUE 18 YEARS

Dana, a probation Officer for 25-years before retiring in 2013, was the one responsible for convincing her husband five years into their marriage to quit his job and become a Deputy Sheriff. She believed in her heart that her husband would enjoy working in this field and turns out she was right. In 2000 Dana's husband followed her prompting to enter Law Enforcement and has been working as a Police Officer ever since.

Nearly two decades later, Dana admits that she still loves watching her husband put on his uniform and badge along with strapping on his duty belt and all that hangs from it. Seeing how her Officer carries himself with an air of respect and how he interacts with inmates have only stirred her admiration for him and the job he performs.

One of the many plus sides for the Law Enforcement couple has been the fact that the Sheriff's department has become one big family. Not just on the job, picking each other up when needed sort of way but on a very personal level.

The sense of true family was felt when their son was only four years old and had to be transported to a Children's

Hospital for emergency surgery. Dana and her husband had to stay in an RV on the premises for the seven days their son spent in the hospital. During that time, a number of Deputies showed their family-like support by taking over her husbands shifts without complaint.

When the couple were finally able to bring their son home,they found that their "department family" had filled their home with get well letters and flowers from the Sheriff himself, to Lieutenant's, Sergeants, custody deputies and more. It was an act of kindness that melted Dana's heart and it has been an act that continues even to this day. Particularly recently when Dana was diagnosed with cancer. The support continually extended from their "department family" has been beautiful and something they will never forget.

Developing strong bonds within the Department has not only made get-togethers fun but has allowed Dana and her husband along with their co-workers to have opportunities to share the good the bad and the really ugly stories that come with a job in Law Enforcement. The ability to share ugly stories such as finding inmates who have committed suicide or fights they've been involved in, blood, cuts, stabbings, or having urine and feces thrown at them without judgement has been invaluable for all of them.

Although Dana could relate to so much about her husband's work in Law Enforcement because of her own career, when it came to being a wife of an Officer and a mother of two, she found herself struggling with many of the same issues other wives behind the blue struggle with.

The loss time with the family, long hours, forced overtime, shifts that needed to be covered at the last minute, missed vacations due to the jail needing 24-hour coverage, missed baseball and football games along with parent teacher meetings and award banquets, all left a definite mark. Despite working in the same field, the demands of the job made it heartbreaking at times for Dana particular when teachers or coaches would ask her if she was a single parent.

Dana recalls one particularly bad argument that seemed to last forever was when she bought four plane tickets and paid the down payment to hold a cabin for a family summer vacation they had planned. Dana and the kids were excited and ready for their family vacation, only to find out that her husband was denied vacation one week before they were set to go due to staff shortage and lack of seniority.

Canceling the vacation, Dana was angry not only at her husband's inability to go but the wasted money. It wasn't one of their better summers as she recalls. However, they managed to work through it with her husband reminding her that one day, he could ask for the time off sooner and he would have the seniority to go. Through the experience Dana began to realize that it wasn't that her husband didn't want to be with the family but it was in fact the job that needed him. She realized that she needed to stop thinking of herself and the kids as second class citizens behind his job. They were first in her husband's life but the fact did remain that his income from the job was necessary to support the family. She knew one day he really would have seniority when it came to vacations, so in the meantime, she needed to be a little more understanding.

Beyond the struggles of missed vacations and family time, one of the greatest challenges for Dana came three years into her husband's job at the jail. A situation arose where Officers tasered an inmate during a scuffle. During the struggle the inmate managed to pull the taser prong out of his leg and jam it into Dana's husband's leg. When it was all over it was determined that the inmate had hepatitis C and AIDS.

Dana along with her husband had to attend a blood borne pathogens class and her husband had to undergo treatment and blood tests for six months to a year. Again, Dana found herself angry at the job as well as herself for recommending it.

Naturally, she was scared for her children and had many questions and concerns. *Did her husband have AIDS? Would her children get AIDS if he kissed them? What about sex? Would she get AIDS?*

For a time Dana let her imagination get the worst of her and it put a terrible strain on their marriage. Fortunately the Health Administrators they dealt with were extremely positive and answered all her questions and concerns. Getting educated about the disease and forcing herself to stop worrying settled her anger and helped her overcome the stress and fear she was feeling.

After two years of testing, Dana offered thanks to God as her husband was declared disease free. Dana remembers well how her husband had seemed strong during the testing process as he mindfully took the pills at the direction of the Doctor and went to all of the appointments with Dana by his side, but in truth he was just as scared as she was. It was a season of intense struggle that Dana would never want to relive but through it all, it made their bond as a married couple stronger.

Despite many challenges, scary times and having to work through a lot of frustration, the good that comes from her husband working in Law Enforcement and knowing his impact with inmates, makes being a wife behind the blue something Dana is proud of.

"My husband talks with inmates about what they were arrested for and how to avoid being arrested again. He has never judged any of them because he knows that's not his job but he has made comments to them about how the revolving door always seems to catch them and bring them back in. He works with some inmates on his crew outside the facility doing clean up and things around the facility and is impressed by some of their abilities. He sees that some of these guys really have talent but how it's been wasted due to drugs or alcohol. But when they are sober they are hard working. Then there are the other inmates he works with that can't read or even tie a knot. The ones who talk about their childhood and why they got into drugs in the first place. My husband says, 'we all walk the same road but some of us just took a wrong path.' So I guess the saying is true, there , but for the grace of God go I."

Through her wide range of experiences Dana gladly offers advice to other wives behind the blue.

A Wife's Advice

1. Communication. Talk, listen and explain how you feel about whatever the issue is. Understand that his job is demanding but that doesn't mean you are second fiddle. It means he is working very hard to keep all the juggled balls in the air and complaining isn't helping. Listen to what he says about the job, be his confidant. He needs to know you will not blab to everyone when he comes home tired and complaining about his job. Let him explain the good, bad and ugly but make sure he understands that you are important too, not by complaining but by explaining that a marriage is two people and even though his job is demanding, you need his shoulder to cry on too.

2. Don't Complain. The children miss him, don't complain to them that daddy is always working and doesn't want to be home with them. Explain to them how important dad's job is and that people need him and his help. Also tell the children how important they are in your life. Don't assume anything, if you don't talk about issues then nothing gets resolved.

3. Most importantly make time for just the two of you. No kids, no other family. Go to the movies or out dancing so you can talk, listen and understand each other.

4. Practice more patience and understanding about his long hours. When the children were young I hated the long hours, I felt like I was doing all the "home" work and he would show up for the good stuff after having fun all day at work "babysitting" inmates. Patience and understanding in this area make things much better.

5. Plan short vacations or get aways to keep the family talking. Believe me when I say he needs to get away from it all just as much as you do, even if it's just a short weekend.

A Wife's Prayer:

Dear God,

Even when I understand that my husband isn't around as much as I want him to be because his demanding job needs him doesn't mean I like it. I often feel left behind, like a second class citizen but that really isn't true. My husband works long, hard hours not to stay away from the family but for the sake of providing for our family. Help me to remember this fact when I'm missing him, again. Teach me how to be more patient and understanding in the areas that I need it most.

My Thoughts:

Open up before God, keep nothing back; he'll do whatever needs to be done: He'll validate your life in the clear light of day and stamp you with approval at high noon.

~Psalms 35:5-6

A Word from Allison Uribe
Author of Cuffs and Coffee

AN UNPREDICTABLE EXPECTATION

Expectation—A word that could bring about the greatest of joys or the sorrow of disappointment. The day I said, "I do", brought so much curiosity. Marriage was one factor, but the understanding that he served and protected the city we resided in, was another. Don't get me wrong, I know I married a man, not a Police Officer. However, the invisible badge he wore each day was a badge that I took on. I accepted it whole heartedly just as I did to the ring he placed on my finger. What would the challenges be? Would this vow for better or worse be carried out? Only time would tell and I couldn't have predicted what would happen.

Looking back, seventeen years later, I am unsure of all I expected this life to be. We are a Law Enforcement family, perhaps as ordinary as any American family. Yet, the badge has changed everything. Perhaps I expected the husband with a nine to five job who came home tired, yet without trauma. I expected the frequent conversations when he arrived home, but silence was far greater. There are times even now, I am not sure I expect anything different from all I have known. But most of all, I am not sure I expect anything different from what I have come to understand. The crazy thing is, I wouldn't change a thing. Sure, this life has brought many surprises, sometimes surprises I would have preferred to pass by. But oh, the strength that has been instilled in us all!

Each time I hold him as he mourns a dead baby, a lifeless body he could not save, or the blood I have washed out of his uniform, strength increases and my skin grows a little thicker. Then, I look in his eyes. In his eyes I can see so much he longs to speak from the depths of his heart, yet the words never come out. How can anyone put into words what a Law Enforcement Officer sees on a daily basis? With little or no time to comprehend or take a breath, they go from one call to another. While I will never see the trauma he sees, I certainly feel it upon his arrival. It's in the drowning sound of his Velcro, the dragging steps on the stairs, the way the front door slams, in the loud sighs of exhaustion, or in the sorrow in his eyes. So much I heard of, but never expected to experience as my own.

Being a wife on duty can be the greatest expectation. Something no single person could ever plan for. Just like the vows we spoke on our wedding day, it's easier said than done. But each day we are given a choice, a choice to say, "I do". Sure, I wanted to leave him so many times, as I hadn't the slightest clue how to be married to a man with a badge. But love, the love I had for him kept me fighting and pushing through. I never could walk out the door, and to this day I praise God I never did. Looking back and learning from all the mistakes we have made, it is with all certainty I can move forward. I can proceed knowing all this life has brought. I can do it with the greatest expectation and greatest of strength. For every trial, sorrowful experience, moments of laughter and celebration, or realizing there are areas in his heart only God can reach, it is well with my soul. While I go about loving the man God placed in my life, I can lean into the promise that God is able to do far and beyond my limited human hands. Long ago, I realized that when I am weak and feel I can't take another step on this thin blue line, I remember God is holding my hand and walking it with me. With all the trauma my husband experiences daily, I know God is able to reach the core of his heart and bring healing. As for me, it is my trust in God that allows me to expect the best, endure the hard, and thrive.

So was this life all I expected it to be? It's probably a mix of yes and no. But with the seventeen years of walking this blue line with him, I can say this: "All along I knew it wouldn't be easy. But even as unpredictable as it was, it is the strength I have gained that exceeded it all."

For more information on Allison Uribe and
Wives on Duty Ministry visit
www.facebook.com/wivesondutyministries

"God found some of the strongest women and made them police wives."

THERESA
A WIFE BEHIND THE BLUE 3 YEARS

When Theresa and her husband first started dating and right on into the beginning years of their marriage, Theresa was under the impression that she was marrying a future high school history teacher. She had no idea that the thought of another career path was brewing in the back of her husband's mind.

Theresa was so certain of her husband's teaching future that when he first told her that he was considering a career in Law Enforcement, she literally laughed at him, assuming he was just trying to get a rise out of her.

Months later when he told her that he honestly could not stop thinking about working in Law Enforcement an immediate peace came over her and she found herself needing to apologize to her husband for initially laughing at him and not taking him seriously. With a peace in her heart, Theresa then told her husband that if indeed it was his calling, then it would be her calling too because she knew that they would be in it together. And there the blue life began.

"By the power of Christ, I felt comfort in his decision to start down his new path. I was able to connect with my aunt and

cousins to get a realistic view of how difficult but rewarding his job (and my job) would be. I expected to go to a lot of events and holidays alone, I expected him to be tired, I expected to hear the crazy stories. From the moment he started applying, I started praying. I knew our faith would play a major role in our success through his career."

Gaining insight on what her role as a wife of an Officer might look like along with knowing her nature as an emotional and passionate person, Theresa began to pray that God would help her to be strong enough in those moments when she needed to be. She became aware of the need to be more selfless and knew she would have to work on the "acts of service" when it came to her husband and so she did, by preparing his clothes, making his lunch, and allowing him time to decompress after long days.

She prepared herself emotionally, mentally and spiritually the best she could in order to transition into the Law Enforcement life. Yet, despite all the preparation, there was one area she wasn't fully prepared for—how quickly she would be affected by the media.

Before I was a Law Enforcement wife, I didn't notice the bashing articles, or the scrutiny, and honestly I didn't notice the deaths of Officers. Now I heard of every single one. I'm still learning that it's okay to "unfriend" people, to look away from comments, to pray when I hear about any deaths or injuries or riots. I became a part of a Law Enforcement Officer's Wife (LEOW) Facebook group over a year ago and that has been life-changing for me. Having women that understand where I am and what my family goes through is amazing. Being able to ask questions or have support from women who have actually been through it is the greatest feeling. We have a yearly conference to meet, hear speakers, and be reminded of the ways we can be there for our husbands and how to help in the best ways when things aren't going well for him. There have been so many things that I've gotten to hear that I never would have thought about to help me be better prepared."

While the couple is fairly new to the blue life, there are two things that Theresa is certain of at this point. One, that this is something her husband is meant to do and the other, a reality check for her, that being a wife behind the blue is a very tough job.

"Most wives don't have the fear of their spouse not coming home from work. Most women don't have to think about where they're going to dinner and who their husband might recognize there. Knowing that if something happened in public, he would run toward it while the rest of us ran away from it. That's a tough realization, and that's our life as Law Enforcement wives."

On a lesser scale of concern yet very relevant for Theresa and her family is the long commute her husband faces daily. While he has a shift that presently works well with the family and he absolutely loves the department he works for, the couple can't help but wonder if one day the long commute and the exhaustion that comes with it, will be too much. At some point her husband, presently working as a Field Evidence Technician as well as SWAT, may need to leave the department he loves and transfer closer to home in order get better rest and also to be able to see their boys sporting events once they start playing sports.

With Theresa's husband having parents who were both teachers and attended every event of his when he was young, it makes it difficult for her husband to imagine not being there himself at his own children's events. The idea of it may just be what he fears the most about his job in Law

Enforcement according to Theresa. Although it's hard for him to imagine not being with his present department, the idea of missing out on some pertinent events with his kids, not just due to his job but made worse by a very long commute is something they realize they may need to address for the family's balance and happiness down the road.

While that is a concern to be addressed in the future, as for now, one of the many things Theresa loves about her husbands job and her role in it, is hearing the stories that her husband tells of people who have come up to him to thank him, or children who look up at him in admiration, and even the way their own boys eyes light up when he walks in the house and answers their daily question of, how many bad guys did you get? These moments bring joy to Theresa's heart as she realizes her husband is blessed as a Peacemaker and it's the very reason that he does what he does.

While the couple haven't experienced too many challenges from the job as of yet, they both realize that in this line of work, challenges are inevitable. Still, there has been a few rough days on the job. Days when Theresa's husband gets off work and instead of his usual routine of going to sleep, he suggests that the family goes out to breakfast or visits the zoo, anything to shake off some of what he has dealt with and seen that day. Such as the days when he has to take a child from their unstable parent or when he tries to convince a woman that she should press charges for the safety of herself and her children. Those days Theresa says, are *the epitome of ugly days*. The ones you can't prepare yourself for and always fear. The ones that you pray wont come, but also know to pray for strength if and when it does.

Still in the early stages of Law Enforcement the couple

are determined to set the proper tone for years to come by drawing wisdom and strength from God, one day at a time as together they fulfill their blue life call. And with that, Theresa offers wisdom way beyond her Law Enforcement Wife years to other wives behind the blue.

A Wife's Advice

1. Keep Christ at the center of your marriage. Pray for your man and pray for your marriage.
2. Read Books. There are awesome books for Law Enforcement families that can really give some insight and good aspects to apply to your life.
3. Make time for yourselves to keep the love alive— Always date your spouse.
4. Discuss ahead of time how much you want your kids to know about daddy's job. Talk about: Why he does it, gun safety, whether or not they should share what their daddy does and how they should or shouldn't respond to negative comments.
5. Be a light. Remind him that there are good people out there still. Caution is great but it's important to remember how much grace and mercy our God shows us daily, and that we may need to show some too.

A Wife's Prayer:

Dear God,

My husband trained hard to be the Officer he is. He studied, practiced, and pursued all that he needed in order to succeed. And now that we are in the Law Enforcement life we need to do the same. We need to study your Word with diligence, practice your principles intentionally and pursue your love with purpose. He may wear the uniform, but we are in this together so help us to continue our training in order to be strong and stay strong in what you've called us both to do.

My Thoughts:

God is a safe place to hide, ready to help when we need him.

~Psalm 46:1

HAILEY
A WIFE BEHIND THE BLUE OVER 30 YEARS

Hailey's husband worked in a correctional and rehabilitation facility for 32 years. While the facility itself has had a long-standing reputation for being violent and dangerous, Hailey's husband didn't necessarily deal with that aspect of it as he worked the majority of his time with minimum and low-security inmates. Starting as a guard, he eventually worked up to the position of Superintendent of one of the prison industries—a furniture fabrication plant, where well-behaved prisoners earned the opportunity to make furniture for tax supported agencies.

Rather untypical for most Law Enforcement wives, Hailey had no real any qualms, or nervous feelings about her husband working in such a facility. Even during times when she knew her husband had to step between aggressive inmates to break up escalating problems, Hailey wasn't inclined towards feelings of fear for her husband on the job.

A big part of being able to maintain a relaxed view of her husband's role in working with inmates was partly because of Hailey's naturally laid back personality and also because when her husband would come home from work each night, he never brought his work home with him. It wasn't a matter of him holding it all in and not revealing things to her, as he definitely would share stories from his day from time to time, but her husband approached his job of overseeing numerous inmates, like he would have any other job. He worked hard, did his best and made every effort to stay positive. This approach to his work in Law Enforcement made it much easier for Hailey to view his job like any other job as well— even if it was in a prison.

In addition to the couple's positive approach to the job, Hailey acknowledges that her greatest help in being at peace with what her husband was doing, was that she relied heavily on God, drew strength from her faith and kept focused on the belief that God had placed her husband in the position he was in for a reason. A position that not only was rewarding for him but for the inmates and in turn for Hailey as well.

Over the years her husband built a strong rapport with a number of the inmates and even had three or four exceptionally close ones who always had his back, whenever anything went down. Such as when some of the "not-so-rehabilitated" inmates would plan something, the inmates that were close to her husband would let him know beforehand. They would warn him without giving away specific names of who was starting what trouble, therefore protecting themselves and Hailey's husband.

Many wives of Officers have gone on ride-alongs or to the gun range to have a better connection and understanding with what their husbands do but for Hailey, it went a bit further.

On various occasions, Hailey's husband took her and their boys to see and meet some of the low-risk inmates that worked directly with him. Hailey recalls what a positive impact it had on her and their boys being able to meeting the inmates. It not only helped them in relating to what he did as part of his job in Law Enforcement, but helped them view some inmates, who had made mistakes but were sincerely working toward change, differently than they would have otherwise.

"They were "lifers" but they were very respectful, to my husband and to me. I think it was because he was really respectful to them and never put them down or made fun of them in front of others. Instead he encouraged them and they respected him for it. Some inmates would even come up to him and say, you've always been good to us."

Hailey shares her memories of two specific "lifers" who were paroled and how she sincerely felt that they were the nicest of men, something you don't typically hear a blue wife say about the inmates her husband has worked with. One of the two men in particular, touched Hailey's heart in a special way.

"He was so nice and when I think about what transpired when he was younger, it just breaks my heart because he was young and quick tempered and that's what landed him in prison. Once he was paroled, my husband and I met with him, took him out to dinner and invited him to our house for the weekend. He went to church with us and we had a very nice time together. He couldn't believe it as we cried and prayed together with him."

With so much good having come from her husband's position in the prison, allowing Hailey to have an overall sense of peace and normalcy within the Law Enforcement life, Hailey admits that it might have been very different for her and her husband had he been on the streets in a police car dealing with all sorts of criminals in various sort of ways.

"The world is so much different today with so much crime. Everyday you're hearing about Police Officers, at least one if not more getting killed. You hear of Officers going to domestic calls and getting hurt, stabbed or worse because of someone else's domestic problems. Maybe because my husband was inside of a prison working with better behaved inmates instead of being out on the streets, having to watch his back all the time and facing a whole different kind of danger, it wasn't as scary for us as it could have been."

Though Hailey didn't have to deal with some of the concerns that other blue wives whose husbands are on the streets deal with, working with inmates locked up for their crimes they committed still presented a measure of danger which fortunately Hailey's husband handled well. His experience as well as Hailey's is a welcomed reminder of the good that can take place from a position in Law Enforcement. Yes, there is ugly in this line of work where laws need to be enforced and many law breakers have no interest for change, but there are also those inmates who really do desire something better for themselves and who truly desire a positive change. For those inmates, having someone in Law Enforcement show them kindness and respect despite their shortcomings as Hailey and her husband both did, can make all the difference.

From her unique experience, Hailey shares two important things with other wives behind the blue, particularly the young wives just starting out.

A Wife's Advice

1. No Fixing! = My husband didn't show a lot of frustration but every now and again he would come home and need to talk. He would need to get the stress of the day out and all I would know to do was listen. I didn't try to fix it because men don't always want you to fix there things, they just want you to listen.

2. Never Forget! = Always remember, especially during challenging times, that God has placed your husband in the position he is in for a reason.

A Wife's Prayer:

Dear God,

Everyone's experiences are different in this line of work. Some better, some worse but you are aware of it all. You have put my husband where you want him to be—not just as an enforcer of the law but as encourager of souls. Whatever the experiences are from day to day for him or for me, help us to remain steadfast in our faith and in the ability to lean on you everyday.

My Thoughts:

Then God was right before him, saying, "I am God...I'll stay with you, I'll protect you wherever you go, and I'll bring you back to this very ground. I'll stick with you until I've done everything I promised you.

~Genesis 28:15

EVELYN
A WIFE BEHIND THE BLUE 9 YEARS

Evelyn's husband was working as a teacher when they were dating and for the first few years of marriage but then the recession hit and teachers were being laid off left and right. Because of the instability for teachers at the time, the couple began to consider how their finances could ever be in a place where they could start a family, especially if Evelyn was to stay home to raise their children.

Her husband had always had an interest in Law Enforcement and as they began to discuss the possibility of a career change over several months, they both felt like it was the best time to pursue it. Since they didn't have children yet, they concluded that if her husband really disliked working in Law Enforcement, he could always go back to teaching as the economy improved. Once the decision was made, Evelyn was excited for the adventure of it all and felt proud that her husband was the type of man willing to do something hard to provide for his family.

In time, the couple stepped into their new blue life with Evelyn having only one real expectation, that people would naturally understand this new life she and her husband were now living. Unfortunately, that was the farthest from the truth. Many friends did not understand the changes taking place in Evelyn's life due to her husband's job and it was a rude awakening.

"I've lost friends over it. I had friends know that I was alone on the holidays and they were totally fine with that. It's been hard for them to understand that when my husband works weekends and is off during the weekdays that means my weekends are lonely while my husband works. And just like how they are busy hanging out with their husbands on the weekends and are available during the weekdays, I'm not available to hang out during the weekdays because I finally have a chance to see my husband."

One would hope friendships would be strong enough when changes come but as many wives of Officer discover, the blue life brings about some changes that others outside of the life just can't relate too, therefore causing, as Evelyn discovered, some friendships to crumble.

Despite the loss of some friendships Evelyn is proud of her husband's career choice. Surprisingly, as time has gone on, Evelyn has found that the good and the bad side to being an Officer of the law can be somewhat of the same thing. As she sees it, the good is all the honor and pride that goes along with her husband serving the community and standing in the face of evil to protect others. While the bad being how the media can negatively portray Officer's serving the community and standing in the face of evil to protect others.

It is certainly challenging for most any loving wife to accept that someone would speak negatively of her husband but with Law Enforcement it becomes the media along with groups of people talking about Officers in a negative way. Saying horrible things without even getting recognition for the many wonderful things Officers do to protect the very people who speak poorly of them is frustrating.

While this is challenging for Evelyn, the greater challenge has been staying connected and on the same page with her Officer especially when it feels like they are living separate lives with separate sleep and awake schedules. For example when Evelyn's husband's schedule doesn't allow him to go with her and their children to church, family events or small groups, she finds it difficult to feel "one" with him because she is doing so many things alone. Thankfully, the couple is determined to work through those kinds of challenges together.

"We've gotten a lot better at prioritizing family time and fig-uring out how to make it work in our family by being creative and doing things like dates during the weekday for breakfast or lunch instead of on the weekends in the evening. We've also just accepted the fact that we need to pay for babysitting for somethings that most people don't have too, in order to make our lives work. For example, I attend a Bible study every Tuesday but if he has to work, we just hire a sitter rather than missing out and feeling bitter about it."

The effort of hiring a babysitter when needed for Bible study in particular has benefited Evelyn and her husband in different ways. For Evelyn, the Bible Study consisting of wives of Officers of all different ages and stages of life has been a huge blessing as she didn't realize until joining a year ago just how much she needed the support. When she walked into the room that first night, she recalls how she didn't have to say anything but just knew that the wives there understood her life.

The benefit for her husband is knowing that his wife is

apart of a strong Bible Study group filled with women of faith who are also wives of Officers. And should anything unfortunate ever happen, his wife would be surrounded by so many women that would help carry her through.

Together, the couple find comfort by being intentional in their efforts to stay connected with one another as well as their Law Enforcement family and other non-Law Enforcement friends who have a good understanding of what the Law Enforcement life is like. The support group that surround them keep them grounded by regularly reminding them that not everyone is like the people Evelyn's husband deals with on a daily basis. In truth there is only a small segment of society that are criminals. This reminder helps both Evelyn and her Officer to move forward one-day-at-a time in all that they are called to do as a blue life family.

After nearly nine years as an Officers wife, Evelyn shares her thoughts with other wives behind the blue.

A Wife's Advice

1. Trust that God loves your husband. Much of my strength comes from God and I trust that He loves my husband more than anyone and has a plan for my husbands life. I also trust that God is good and will carry us through any dark valley.

2. Be Intentional. Surround yourself with people you can be honest with when life is hard, that can help when needed and even give you creative ideas on how to work on your marriage.

3. Remember that your husband can't read your mind. Tell him your needs. For me, if my husband thought I was okay, it was easy for him to take on overtime assignments or work later to help someone out. But if I had been clear in communicating that I was struggling on the home front and needed him home, he would have been quicker to get there.

4. Don't expect people who don't live in this reality to understand. You will have to explain, sometimes more than once the type of life you now lead as a blue family. Some will come to understand and others won't.

5. Venting is healthy. Sometimes as a wife of an Officer you just need to vent and get the demands of his job off your chest. Venting is healthy, but just be careful who you vent too.

A Wife's Prayer:

Dear God,

There really are more good people in this world than bad but sometimes the media and even a few unhappy people can often stir up a lot of negative thoughts. Help me to focus on the good. Give my husband and I a strong support system of friends and family who will keep us grounded and remind us on those harder days when we struggle to feel connected, that despite those "feelings," we are always connected with you and with that, we can stay connected with each other.

My Thoughts:

The person in right standing before God through loyal and steady believing is fully alive, really alive.

~Habakkuk 2:4

No Boys Allowed!
EXCEPT ADAM DAVIS

When I first began discussing the idea for this book with my husband, he wondered if I was going to be writing about all the police guy stuff. You know, the taking down of criminals, sharp shooting, SWAT, arrests, crimes, tactical gear, the brotherhood of Officers and the odd survival-like humor that develops between Officers. And while I'm sure my husband would have enjoyed a book like that, I was quick to explain that *Wives Behind the Blue* wasn't that kind of book. My exact words were, "No, No, It's a girls club—No boys allowed!"

I explained that *Wives Behind the Blue* would be a place where a number of beautiful women would share what it's like being a wife of an Officer, period.

My husband chuckled over the *girls club-no boys allowed* comment, but saying it that way expressed the clear direction for the book. Though all of the stories would include things about our husbands and police guy stuff, ultimately it would be *our* book, our feelings, thoughts, expectations and experiences. Indeed it would be a book for wives behind the blue.

As I worked through this book, I had every intention of

sticking with the "No Boys Allowed!" rule, only sharing the voices of women, until I came across an article written by Adam Davis called *6 Traits of a Bulletproof Police Marriage*. The article spoke to me in a special way and caused me to reconsider the "No Boys Allowed!" rule

A former Law Enforcement Officer, Adam Davis now serves those who walk the thin blue line, and their loved ones, through various speaking engagements, articles, blogs, his website as well as through his books, *Behind the Badge: 365 Daily Devotions for Law Enforcement* and *Bulletproof Marriage: a 90 Day Devotional.*

As I read *6 Traits of a Bulletproof Police Marriage* something really stuck with me. While the article is geared toward Officers who are married, it made me pause and think how I could apply these traits to my role as a wife and better bulletproof my marriage even after 25 years.

Most of the traits mentioned in his article are also mentioned throughout the various stories shared in this book but hearing it from a man's perspective was a nice change. And a reminder that what we as wives desire from our Officers is also something we need to give our Officers. Unless you are in Law Enforcement yourself, as a wife your role is obviously different then your husbands, but regardless, as wives we still can apply these traits ourselves.

So yes, *Wives Behind the Blue* is still a "A girls club" kind of book but let's make one exception with Adam Davis and take a look at what this one-time Officer advices other Officers to do in order to bulletproof their police marriage and lets see what we as wives, might take from it.

6 TRAITS OF A BULLETPROOF POLICE MARRIAGE
REPRINTED WITH PERMISSION BY ADAM DAVIS

If you are currently or have been married, you know it's tough work. If you want to have a successful and peaceful marriage, understanding the importance of forgiveness and communication is critical.

My wife and I were married at a very young age. I packed my bags about 12 times during the first year of our marriage. I was a horrible husband. In the first several years of our marriage, I held around seven different jobs. I was unstable, uncommitted, extremely immature and ill-prepared for marriage.

After several years, I began to settle down. I didn't settle down because I found my "dream job." Rather, I settled down because I became a father, and I realized my wife and child's lives were more important than my own. I survived marriage because of the love my wife showed me. She was forgiving and I was forgiving. When problems arose, they were mainly because of miscommunication or lack of communication. Once I learned my passion, understood how I was created and why, life became a little clearer for me.

Tie these issues into the stress of one or both spouses being in Law Enforcement and you will quickly see the reason for so many marriage dissolutions in the profession.

Many couples live under loads of tremendous debt, constant stress, busy schedules and tons of activities for the kids. So how can we have lasting marriages? Here are some ways I revolutionized my marriage.

1. PRIORITIZE COMMUNICATION

We realize the importance of communicating with our superiors, peers and community at a professional level. How do you feel about communication with your spouse? Communication should be number one, two, three, four and five on this list. It is truly critical to relationships.

Not merely communicating, but how we communicate with our spouse is vital. When we communicate with hate, resentment or jealousy, we are ineffective. When we have a bad day on the job, we should remember to take time and cool down before interacting with our family.

2. BE PRESENT

You may be asking, "What in the world does this mean?" It means when you are with your spouse, be in the moment. Put the smartphone and tablets down. Return your emails, messages and calls later.

Look at your spouse as your teammate. Your time is already stretched thin, so when you are with your spouse, be with your spouse.

3. NEVER STOP PURSUING YOUR SPOUSE

Always pursue your spouse. Send your spouse texts. Comment on your spouse's beauty. Praise him or her in public. Hold your spouse's hand. Hold the door open. I could go on, but, you get the drill.

Your spouse wants you to continue this pursuit. They don't

want to feel like trophies that were won in a contest. Never. Stop. Dating. Ever.

4. TREAT YOUR SPOUSE WITH KINDNESS

You've heard the saying, "Do unto others as you would have them do unto you." This applies to marriage as well. Kindness is a rare quality nowadays, and it's easy to take someone we love for granted.

Show your spouse kindness, respect and love. When he or she performs some act of kindness to you, show your appreciation. Kindness shows you have a concern for your spouse. Trust me when I say, you will not regret showing kindness. It is easy to dismiss the need for this when we are continually around negativity, evil and hate. Don't allow your day to contaminate the kindness your spouse deserves.

5. FORGIVE FREELY

I have been on both sides of this issue. We should be free to forgive our spouses as we would want someone to be free to forgive us. Everyone makes mistakes – I have learned this lesson the hard way.

6. MAINTAIN BALANCE

When you go on duty, leave the stuff from home at home. I am talking about the money problems, the argument you had with your spouse, the plans for the upcoming weekend. Focus on your duty to make it home at the end of your shift and to ensure your brothers and sisters make it home as well.

In the same light, however, when you prepare to go off duty at the end of shift, leave what happened at work at work. Your family doesn't deserve to be the punching bag for the mess you dealt with on duty.

You could choose to be intimidating, refuse to cooperate, negotiate, or compromise, but your spouse may not wait on you to change forever. Focus on loving your spouse. Focus on why you are doing what it is you are doing. If you are going to experience any level of success in your career and relationship, you will have to establish a fine balance between the two of them, or one—or both—will destroy you.

For more information on Adam Davis visit
www.TheAdamDavis.com.

"You wouldn't understand unless the sound of Velcro makes you relax."

BARBARA
A WIFE BEHIND THE BLUE 28 YEARS

Barbara's husband served as a deputy for nine years, worked in the jail and on patrol for four before making a lateral transfer to another county. There he served as a Field Training Officer, a canine Officer and also served on the Street Gang Unit before retiring after twenty-eight years of service.

Barbara notes that out of all of his experiences, his happiest years in Law Enforcement where the fifteen years spent as a canine Officer. In fact, he was able to take the experience into his retirement as he is currently working with a Canine and Consulting Company.

Meeting in college years ago, Barbara says she had a pretty good understanding early on that her husband longed for a career as a Police Officer. Despite knowing this desire, Barbara struggled with him wanting to be an Officer for two main reasons. The crime in the urban community they lived in was (and still is) pretty significant so the idea of her husband serving as a Police Officer in that community was a bit scary for her. Another reason Barbara was hesitant to accept her husbands Law Enforcement dream was because at the time that he submitted his application to the Sheriff's

Department, he was working for an aircraft manufacturer which was a substantial job for someone so young.

It was hard to process at first but eventually it became very clear to Barbara that her husband was made to be a protector therefore being a Police Officer was indeed a perfect job for him. One that could take his strengths and allow him to use them in a positive way. She also realized that despite her concerns her role as his wife was to support him in his decision to pursue a career. Even if that career was in Law Enforcement.

Being just twenty years old when they married and her husband began his Law Enforcement career helped the young couple define their expectations as they went along verses having them set in stone from the start, which often causes problems for couples.

One thing that proved helpful for young Barbara was having had many examples of people in her life who were hard workers and loved what they did as a career. So as her husband entered into Law Enforcement wholeheartedly, Barbara felt comfortable with his level of dedication to it. Understanding his commitment to hard work helped a great deal, particularly when their children came along. Barbara knew she would be the primary caregiver and didn't harbor resentment because of her husband's commitment to his demanding job. On the contrary, having a hard working husband who loved his career was the norm and made her proud.

Still, there were times when Barbara felt frustrated with what she thought was a lack of engagement by her husband in their day to day life as the job went on. In retrospect, she now understands that it was simply his way to function as a Police Officer, husband and a dad. Shutting her and their children out on occasion was a defense mechanism he had developed to protect them. It may not have been necessarily the best or healthy method but it was a way for him to keep moving forward. Barbara admits, it wasn't perfect but perfection wasn't the point, progress was.

Being certain that she and her husband were intended for this Law Enforcement life helped Barbara progress through the rough patches, the late nights, the missed family functions, and even the disengaging and shutting down from her Officer from time to time. Believing they had a greater purpose in the blue life, kept them moving forward and purposefully pressing on.

Reflecting on the many years of the Law Enforcement life, Barbara admits she is still proud of the fact that her husband chose a career that focuses on serving others and for all his years of service, she had confidence in his ability to do his job and do it well. He took his responsibility to protect and serve seriously and part of that responsibility was coming home safe to his family every night. Yet the knowledge that her husband could have either taken a life or given his life in an act of serving others did cause some sleepless nights and worry for Barbara. It was a profound responsibility that weighed heavy on both of their hearts.

Barbara admits that her husband's career has often reminded her of the old adage, *our strengths can also be our biggest challenge.*

My husband will always be a vigilant protector. With that said, I am included in the category of needing to be protected which does not always lend to open communication and totally rubs up against my independence. As we all know honest and open communication is key to a healthy marriage. I would like to say we mastered this lesson early on in our marriage, unfortunately or fortunately that was not the case. We are still working on this lesson every day and I think it is our stubbornness or persistence and commitment to each other that helps us to learn and forgive when we have misunderstandings. Also I have found it very helpful to re-frame a situation and look at it in the spirit that is given or focus on the positive instead of the delivery. For example, I choose to see my husband's need to always sit in a place where he has the best vantage point (no back to the door) as a way to protect our family and not be annoyed by what appears to be a very controlling attitude.

Having a willingness to re-frame situations along with a commitment to support her husband regardless of the situation, has helped Barbara's husband know that even when she is at her angriest, her commitment to their family and to him never wavers. Likewise, her husband's commitment to Barbara and their family and his willingness to support her in accomplishing her dreams, has helped the couple balance each other out and keep them grounded in not only married life but the blue life.

Having spent three decades as a wife of an Officer Barbara shares some practical advice for other wives behind the blue.

A Wife's Advice

1. Know that you are equipped to handle this experience. Trust and have faith in God's divine plan. You got this!
2. Try to not take life too seriously; laughing is good for the soul, especially laughing with each other.
3. Have open and honest communication even when it is difficult.
4. Remember to forgive yourself and your husband for being imperfect human beings while trying to make this thing called marriage work in our everyday life.
5. Always stay hopeful because tomorrow is a new day.

A Wife's Prayer:

Dear God,

Teach me how to re-frame words or actions when need be between my husband and myself. Point me toward the positive instead of always assuming the worst when we are not on the same page. And while my husband's role is serious and so is mine as his wife, help us both learn how to not take life too seriously all the time, leaving room for a bit more laughter.

My Thoughts:

Light, space, zest—that's God! So, with him on my side I'm fearless, afraid of no one and nothing.

~Psalm 27:1

LUCY
A WIFE BEHIND THE BLUE 10 YEARS

Before becoming an Officer, Lucy's husband participated in an Explorer program which teaches youth different aspects of Law Enforcement. Starting the program at sixteen, he worked his way up to Explorer Captain and at twenty-one went straight into the Police Academy.

It was during the Academy that Lucy first became friends with her husband and attended his graduation a few months before they actually started dating. Once they began to officially date Lucy says she was supportive and encouraging of his Law Enforcement interest but really had no clue as to what or how the choice her friend (soon to be boyfriend, then fiancé' then husband) had already made would impact her life.

She admits to having no real clue as to what it would really mean being a blue wife or how it would change, or seem so different from her other friends and their relationships and marriages. She simply assumed her marriage and the lifestyle of being a Law Enforcement family would be easy. She thought it would be full of great communication and that it would look like how it had been when they were dating. Looking back, she knows she was wrong.

Recalling how it was when they were dating Lucy tells of how her husband would stay up and talk with her on the phone instead of going to bed when he was tired. They would spend as much time together as they possibly could even though the stress level was high as he had just finished up his probation and was in the process of completing his Field Training Officer requirements. Still despite the high stress, as a young dating a couple they found a way to make it work.

Before getting married, Lucy did a ride-a-long which she says was a great way to see her Officer for who he was and helped her understand a bit more of why he did some of the quirky things that he did.

Although she made every effort to learn more about her future husband and his career choice and had a positive outlook on their upcoming marriage, Lucy admits, that her own tough upbringing left her with little idea as to what a healthy marriage was supposed to look like, let alone a blue marriage. The only thing Lucy knew for sure is that her marriage had to be better than what she had been shown while growing up.

After getting married, she knew her husband wouldn't be home every night and that they wouldn't always be sleeping in the same bed at the same time which was very different than any of her friends marriages, but she never pictured it to be as difficult as it was.

Hardly seeing each other, especially in the very beginning of their marriage and no longer really dating each other because of conflicting schedules was extremely challenging, more so because there wasn't anything that they could really do to change it. It was just all part of the job so they just had to deal with it and learn how to work through it which took a lot of time.

Right after we got married, my husband was placed on grave-yard shift right away. I was terrified to be home alone. Not that anything had ever happened or I had anything to be afraid of but I would come home from work, eat dinner, and barricade myself upstairs in our bedroom with a chair next to the door to take a quick shower because I couldn't even close my eyes while shampooing my hair. Then I would get ready for bed and stay in our bedroom with my cat for the rest of the night, watching T.V. or Netflix until I fell asleep. It took a whole year just to get used to being by myself at night. I wasn't worried about him while he was working I was just worried about me, being home alone, because it was a new experience, it was lonely and I had to get used to it. Having a cat helped and I slowly got braver and braver.

For a long time, we lived like roommates instead of husband and wife, because he worked while I slept and I worked while he slept. He had already left for work before I got home from work. We just bypassed each other. And when he was on his days off, he was sleeping for half the day because that is what his body needed. It was so difficult. Our communication with each other was unloving, disrespectful and awful towards each other and our expectations got in the way, (maybe more my expectations of our relationship than his).

God used that time in our lives to grow us, mature us and grow our marriage stronger. We had to make some changes in our relationship and learn how to communicate respectfully, lovingly, and fully, instead of just part way. We had to learn to be unselfish of what each of us wanted or needed. And we are still learning how to communicate in this way.

Hitting rock bottom in our marriage, divorce was never a

question or an option for us, we were completely committed to each other and wanted to start putting in the work. Communication is hard enough in a brand-new marriage but add in the career of Law Enforcement and it just gets that much tougher with little communication at times. God met us where we were, at the end of our rope, and we decided to work through it. To put the hard work in and not ever give up. We took a hard look at all extra pieces of the job that were added that didn't need to be and decided to pull back on some of them. We had to prioritize our relationship over the badge and all that came with it. Our life, our relationship, our family, had to come first.

There were so many eggs in one basket, too many and we needed to take some of those eggs out. Which for us, meant switching to day shift since the seniority was there and it was an option, it meant giving up other things. It meant stepping down from some special assignments from work or not saying yes to certain ones that were offered. We also had to step back from trying to always say "yes" to everything and everyone and learn to say "no" when needed.

It wasn't until five or six years down the road into our marriage that we discovered how much our lives were really different or effected by his career. The long hours and days as well as the amount of calls he had been a part of, the things running through his head on a daily basis were definitely catching up with him and waring on us. He was stressed a lot of the time and exhausted. He started to become trapped in our own home because it was the only place he felt completely comfortable and he didn't want to go or do anything except sit in his chair and watch TV and movies or research things on his phone but not really engage in anything except the kids.

It didn't really feel like we had a relationship we were just *living as roommates and at the time it felt like I was taking care of everything and he was just working.*

As challenging as those first few years were, Lucy and her husband hit a real slump when he was the first to respond to a particular call. It was the hardest call he had been on thus far. That call also started releasing other hard calls that he had been a part of and that he had stuffed and didn't handle the right way. At the time, Lucy's husband didn't feel that he could talk about what he was experiencing with her and so he opted to shut down in efforts to protect her.

At this point, the couple had children and the only thing Lucy knew about whatever her husband was going through was that he had placed his kids terrified faces at the scene he came upon in his mind and couldn't get those images out of his head. It was something we had never walked through before and it was overwhelming.

Lucy tells of how the hyper-vigilant trait, known to plague Officers was a real thing for her husband at this point and it was affecting their family and their lives. Fortunately, the saving grace came when her husband was assigned to go to an *Emotional Survival course by Kevin M. Gilmartin, Ph.D.*

After attending the course, he came home with a sense of hope and encouragement, feeling validated that he wasn't the only one who was walking through what he was feeling. He opened up and explained to Lucy what his body physically goes through after a shift—an adrenaline high on high functioning alert all day for every call then physically hitting rock bottom when he got home. It was the complete opposite end of the pendulum swing everyday but he learned it was normal and that he had to work extra hard to fight against the deep crash he experienced daily in order to level out.

It wasn't impossible but it required work. So the couple started reading, *Emotional Survival for Law Enforcement by Kevin M. Gilmartin, Ph.D.* together and began to implement some of the small changes to help combat the emotional lows.

The first thing they implemented was exercising and eating right which they learned was so important because it relieves stress and it helps release cortisol.

The second thing they learned together was that if her husband didn't want to get up out of his chair to go outside, he was supposed to force himself to do it anyway. Not in a nagging sense but because he desperately wanted to change.

The most important thing that they took away from the book was that it wasn't wrong that her husband was feeling the way he did and that he wasn't alone.

Once they started implementing the ideas shared in the book along with her husband seeking out help from a Police Chaplin within his department, Lucy started seeing her Officer come out of the slump. It was then that they were able to reconnect and realize the importance of making their relationship a priority.

When asked how Lucy and her husband help keep each other grounded now after many years in the blue life, she says by reminding him that the whole world is not corrupt, only the small percentage that he deals with. She reminds him to keep his heart soft in certain areas and that there really are people in the community who appreciate all that he does and are thankful for the work and the sacrifice he makes each day. Lucy also makes every effort to provide a home that he wants to come home to when his shift is over. Not perfectly picked up or clean all the time but a peaceful home, even with four little ones.

On the other hand, Lucy's husband helps her stay grounded by reminding her when she is feeling stressed or overwhelmed from overtime hours, not coming home on time, court dates and single parenting through it all that God put them together because they're meant to be together. With a kiss on the forehead and a tight hug, he often reassures Lucy that just as God has designed him to be a Police Officer, He has also designed her to be a support to him and to the children and to withstand all that it entails because God has given her everything she needs to be a wife and mother to the best of her ability. Not perfect, but with God's help, the absolute best she can be.

Lucy is grateful that her husband, now in the position of Financial and Property Crimes Detective, brings the calming presence he has learned to implement at work when dealing with all sorts of people, into their marriage helping her stay grounded and is beyond grateful for all the growth they have both experienced over the years in their blue line marriage. And with all that experience she shares valuable wisdom in some key areas with other wives behind the blue.

A Wife's Advice

1. Start your day in God's Word. Starting my day in God's word is the only way I can stay strong while supporting my husband. To be surrendered to Him, keeping my focus on Jesus throughout my day leaning into the spirit and listening for guidance, encouragement and truth rather than allowing temptations and lies of the enemy to beat me up all day long. When I fix my eyes on Jesus a joy washes over me and my responses to my husband's late-night shifts or change of schedule is entirely different than the negative response that it might be otherwise.

2. Take care of yourself. If you are not taking care of yourself then you can't take care of anyone else. It has taken me at long time to figure that out.

3. Make your relationship a priority. Date each other and be open. Communicate about our day, import-ant issues, your desires and dreams. Don't loose each other amongst the chaos but enjoy the journey not just try to get through it. Besides when the career is ended and the kids are grown and moved out, in the end it will just be us and we want those days to be so sweet, loving each other more than ever and it starts by building that long lasting relationship now.

4. Meet him at the door. Something new I am doing is to be the first to the door to greet him when he comes home from anywhere not just work. Sometimes it's really tough because I'm cooking dinner, or changing a diaper, or in the middle of disciplining our children, but I try because it lets him know he is valued and

cherished and wanted and it seems to set the tone for the rest of the day or evening.

5. Write it out. Once when I was feeling extremely bitter and angry about getting "the call" that my husband was yet again going to be late due to work when I came across a quote that felt like a straight knock in the teeth.

"Strong women don't play victim, don't make themselves look pitiful, and don't point fingers. They stand and they deal."

~Mandy Hale.

I had to learn and train myself to not play the victim, to not listen to my feelings and emotions and let them run wild, and to not allow "the call" to derail me because it was. It really was.

I decided to try something new. I wrote out my own Pity Party—a pretend scenario of what would happen when I would get "the call" and everything that would play out in my head and what I was going to do about it. Would I wallow in it or accept it and grow from it?

I've included a Pity Party I wrote out as an example for the process I went through.

LUCY'S PITY PARTY

My phone rings. It's my husband at work. Calling to tell me he won't be home for dinner, he got stuck on a very late call for the third night in a row this week. He says, "I'm not sure how long, but I'll try to keep you updated as best as I can."

The next day is his day off. We were supposed to pack the kids up and get out of town for some fun. Now not knowing when he will be getting off and knowing full well he will need to sleep after his shift who knows how it will all play out. All these phrases start running through my head after he hangs up the phone with me:

What Time?

I already started packing everything for the next day—the lunches, snacks, extra clothes and diaper bag. I am prepared, now this gets thrown at me.

Are we even going?

There goes dinner as a family around the table again.

Why can't we just have a normal family, with normal job hours?

Why us?

Why do I have to break the news to my kids again that things may not go according to plan?

Bitterness, Resentment, Anger, Disappointment, and Frustration all start to set in.

Now not only do we have to do dinner alone again, I don't even want to cook anymore. Oatmeal/Peanut butter it is. Forget about cooking dinner. Oh yeah, it's been a really rough day for me, screaming, yelling, lack of obedience-all day and naps skipped. I'm at the end of my rope, and now…I'm on my own again.

Here I am having to put the kids to bed without a goodnight kiss from Daddy because they haven't even been able to see him in the last three days. My heart is breaking for them. The hardest part of my day is bedtime, with no back-up.

I can't do this without you God. I don't want to be angry. Help me to understand this isn't being done to me, it isn't not my husband's fault. He isn't doing this on purpose, he would much rather be here with me right now. But he is providing for our family, and you are using him in your kingdom. Lord help me turn my heart back to you. Back to gratitude instead of resentment and bitterness. Help me to see beyond the circumstances I face at this very moment.

Today, right now, lift me up, encourage me, strengthen me and lift up my weary head. Give me the endurance and passion to finish this race well. Use me to speak to my kids and use me as an example. Rescue their hearts.

As I sit in an empty house or go to bed alone help me to not play the comparison game in my head (how so and so's husband is home for dinner every night). Don't allow the enemy to have a foothold on my heart, feelings, or emotions. Help me to be attuned to your voice to hear you and your encouragement and wisdom for me. Help me to stay present, to feed my soul instead of soaking in pity, wallowing in chocolate. Help me not get sucked into T.V. or social media but instead choose something more life-giving such as a podcast, painting, crafting, crocheting, music, a bath, journaling, or praying for my husband.

Thank you that I was able to have communication with him and to have the ability to know that he isn't going to be able to come home on time. Lord keep him safe, as he goes about the rest of his evening. Thank you for the man he is and the way he is leading our family, the kids, and our marriage. Thank you for bringing him into my life to complete me, not to fill me, but to be my other half.

Provide him the endurance, stamina, wisdom, discernment, safety, and encouragement he needs to continue and finish out the rest of the day strong as he is exhausted too, not just me. May you use him in the department to glorify you and further your kingdom.

You are so gracious to us. Be with all of us tonight protecting us and keeping us safe."

As I took the time to write out what would actually go through my head I was legitimately getting angry and bitter at first and it was just a fake scenario. But the best part of writing it out was that I was able to see how my bitterness turned to thankfulness, gratitude and joy for my husband when I turned my heart to God and allowed him to work in me.

I encourage you to write out your own Pity Party if need be. Write out how it plays out for you, what thoughts or lies go through your head so you can begin to recognize when those thoughts creep in and take them captive and put an end to them, cancel them, and shut them down. It was extremely helpful for me and I hope it will be for you too.

A Wife's Prayer

Dear God,

Remind me as often as I need it that I am totally and completely capable of being who you've created me to be and doing all that you've called me to do.

My Thoughts:

Don't turn your back on God. Worship and serve him heart and soul.

~1 Samuel 12:22

Una
A WIFE BEHIND THE BLUE 18 YEARS

When her husband first realized this was the direction he wanted to go, he was afraid to tell Una for fear of what her response might be. He knew that some wives might not take it well if their husband's said they wanted a career that included putting their life on the line on a regular basis so he kept quiet about it at first. Una however, knew something was on her husband's mind and when she finally got it out of him, learning that he wanted to join the Police Academy and have a career as a Law Enforcement Officer, she was completely supportive of his choice. Here her husband had assumed she might be overly worried about his safety and not want him in this particular line of work, but was pleasantly surprised to discover how excited she truly was that he found something he would love to do.

As for her concern for her husband's safety, Una had settled in her mind long before the idea of Law Enforcement that her husband's safety and ultimately his life was in God's hands, not theirs. No job choice would ever change that.

Una had a good understanding from the start that a position in Law Enforcement meant danger, long hours, and missed family events and so she simply chose to embrace it.

When her husband started his training, his routine consisted of getting up, driving to the Academy, coming home, polishing, shining and ironing his uniform and equipment, then packing his lunch, and going straight to bed. There was no extra time in the day for Una and the kids during those months. Therefore, Una concluded right away that the best thing for her and the success of her now twenty-four years of marriage was to be her own person. She knew she had to be independent of her husband until he was free to be with her. Eighteen years of Law Enforcement life later, this approach is still working.

Upon graduating the Academy Una's husband began working the night shift consisting of twelve hour days, three to four nights a week. By choosing not to have expectations of her husband during the times he worked, much of the pressure that would have otherwise been there for both of them was removed. Making the times when he wasn't working and could be present with her and the children an added bonus.

Having opposite schedules, Una recalls how their bed was never made up because one of them was always in it. While she rightfully could have focused on the fact that she and her husband rarely shared the same bedtime, she chose to focus more on the fact that she really did enjoy having the whole bed to herself when she slept, just as much as he did.

Eventually her husband transferred to days and they were finally able to share the same bedtime for the most part, as he had an early bedtime of 7:30pm and needed to be up by 3am. Una admits that regardless of the shift her husband had, the bigger challenge was trying to keep the house quiet while he slept. This was no easy task with the couples six children.

As with most Law Enforcement wives, Una planned the majority of activities without her husband, making every effort to keep their family life as normal as possible. Not wanting to draw attention to the fact that her husband had to miss some milestones or special occasions, whenever there was an event or birthday he missed, Una would make the effort of taking really great pictures and videos, sending them to her husband via text or email to enjoy. When he would arrive home after the event had occurred, he would make a big deal out of seeing the pictures and videos of the milestones and made a point to spend special time, even briefly, with each and every one of them. He would engage the children with excitement and they responded likewise, recounting every detail of the event joyfully with him. This routine played an important part of keeping Una's husband plugged in with the kids as well as keeping their relationship strong.

Another important part to Una's success as a wife behind the blue has been the fact that both sets of in-laws have helped with vacations, activities and parties, particularly when the demands of the job kept her husband away. Because of their extended love and support, Una's children basked in the attention they were given and never had a sense of longing as their physical and emotional needs were being met.

Una has been determined from day one to embrace the challenges of living the blue life with a positive and grateful attitude. She has taken the many challenges that arise as a wife of an Officer, let alone a mother of six, all in stride and for the most part has been successful at doing so. However, there are a few areas of Law Enforcement that Una admits are disappointing and difficult to take in stride. The first being the politics associated with being an Officer.

Watching society beg for an Officer's assistance and then watching those same people lash out in anger at the police in general is upsetting. As with many involved in the blue life, Una never expected to see as she did a couple years ago, where Officers had to watch their backs for fear of someone in society randomly lashing out at them.

Another challenging area for Una is the fact that when something happens to someone at the Sheriff's office, the department / agency moves on without the person. Their role is absorbed by others and after a short while, it seems that they were hardly missed. Seeing this unpleasant reality play out has been an important reminder for Una and her Officer that no job is eternal but people are. And whether one is a Police Officer or not, the job never defines the person.

While convincing society to maintain a positive view of Law Enforcement Officers and not letting the job define you is a hard task, Una recalls a time when she and her husband had the difficult task of convincing well-meaning family members that their personal blue life was all good.

"My husband had been an Officer for about ten years and family members commented on never seeing him at family events. My extended family began asking questions about the security of our relationship. We assured them that we were fine. Apparently not believing us they asked our parents about our relationship and our parents also assured them that we were fine. Not believing them either, they finally staged an intervention led by my aunt and grandmother about the status of our relationship. My husband and I had to explain our plan and logic. It was his choice to either work overtime, on a holiday and miss a family event or

not. Because holiday pay is worth much more than regular pay and being that the kids would be entertained by other family members during those events, he would usually take the time to work. They nodded like they understood but I'm not sure that they believed us. I think they secretly believed we had divorced.

After that intervention we made sure that my husband attended some events throughout the year. They still gave us the stink-eye for a couple years, [assuming there was trouble in paradise] but eventually they come around."

Embracing her role as a wife behind the blue from the start and trusting God every step of the way even during the family intervention, Una feels that their Law Enforcement life has been exactly as one might expect. Long hours, hard work, missed activities and a lot of compromise, but through it all, she considers all that her Officer is and does to be priceless.

Having almost two decades of experience as an Officer's wife, Una shares some advice for other wives behind the blue.

A Wife's Advice

1. Remember that God is your source, not your husband or his department.
2. Play together, pray together, attend church / bible studies together and laugh together.
3. Try not to have any expectations of your husband when he is working. If he needs to stay late, place his dinner aside and move on with your night. If he misses something, fill him in later. If he needs to go into work, encourage him to go do what he does.
4. Find a way to marry your different interests and activities. For example: I like Scuba Diving but my husband hates cold, shark infested waters. But he does like kayaking so he often kayak's above while I dive below.
5. Give him space, support and peace until he is ready to talk. Make yourself available to talk and try not to overreact to what he has experienced. Sometimes all you can do is be there with a loving embrace as he deals with the terrible things in his own way.

A Wife's Prayer

Dear God,

Choosing to embrace something doesn't mean it will always be easy but it does mean I don't have to fight so hard against the challenges and changes coming my way. With your power and your strength help me embrace my husband's position as a Law Enforcement Officer and all the challenges that come with it. Help me also to embrace my role as his wife with love, support and understanding.

My Thoughts:

Even when the way goes through Death Valley, I'm not afraid when you walk at my side. Your trusty shepherd's crook makes me feel secure.

~Psalm 23:4

ELLA
A WIFE BEHIND THE BLUE 25 YEARS

Ella was 19 years old when she began dating her husband. She knew from the start that he wanted a career in Law Enforcement. At the time, being young and in love, she considered his career of Law Enforcement to be a "hero" position. Although unsure of what the Police life would bring her, she was excited about the possibilities and had many amazing expectations for what her marriage would be like.

I did, at that young age, know Jesus and prayed about it. I knew that it would be different, whatever that meant. During pre-marital counseling our pastor talked to us about the high divorce rate in Law Enforcement, and his concerns. It was brought to my awareness, and I paused to consider, do I really want to do this? But in reality, I was too young and in love to even consider not living this life with the man I loved.

Just barely out of her teens, Ella married her future Law Enforcement Officer without fear or concern. She felt nothing but happiness and gratitude knowing that she married a good man who had a strong career ahead of him and would take care of her and their future family.

I was not a fearful wife, even at a young age. I had my own education and career that I was focused on as well. Even though I wasn't beginning a career outside of the home until later on in my life, I was working hard on achieving my education and then two years into our marriage we started having our family.

While Ella focused on her new family, her husband joined the Academy and began his career as an Officer. She wanted her husband to have the freedom to grow as a man and as an Officer so she completely supported him and was never overly involved in his career to the point of micromanaging him or stressing over the nature of the job.

As the type of person who doesn't mind being alone, Ella adjusted quickly to the odd shifts and the need for overtime without much concern. That is until later when they had children—one girl, one boy followed by triplets boys.

Having five children to care for suddenly made the varying shifts and long hours away a bit more stressful. Fortunately for Ella, her husband knew how to give her the attention she needed when he was around. Thanks to the example of his own father who always put his wife first while also pursuing a career in Law Enforcement, Ella's husband had a strong sense of loyalty and the know-how to keep his marriage a top priority.

Even still, there were times when he did not clue-in to Ella's needs, when the well known hyper-vigilance of the job got in the way. Those times led to many talks, and even some intense arguments about working together as a couple. Thankfully having a strong foundation in faith, helped them work through those hard and difficult times.

By the time their triplets started kindergarten Ella went back to school and eventually earned a nursing degree. As her children got older, she began working at a medical center for eight years and now she works at a state prison. Pursuing her own education, working in a field she enjoys along with raising her children and having strong faith has better equipped Ella in supporting her husband, now working in the position of a detective.

After all these years being a part of the blue life as a blue wife, Ella still considers her husband's work as an Officer as a "hero" position despite the many marks left by the job.

Whether on the gang task force or in other units, some of the marks came about by things such as when Ella's husband fell out of a second story window and injured his back while on duty, or battling the media and their continued hate for Law Enforcement or being in the middle of riots, fearing for his life. More than once Ella has held her broken-hearted husband as he cried over an abused child or a SIDS baby. Or struggled to inform her of yet another co-worker getting a divorce, or one that has committed suicide.

All these incidences, risks that are a part of an Officer's daily job, have left its mark on her husband's heart and on Ella's. But none as much as when Ella and her husband received a call two years ago letting them know that her husband's brother, also a Deputy, was killed in the line of duty.

Ella's brother-in-law's tragic and heroic death has left a huge void in their family. Nonetheless, the couple has chosen not to live under the umbrella of pain and sadness. On the day his brother died, Ella's husband said something that not only reflected his heart over the loss of his brother but perhaps reflects the hope in the heart of our men in blue and why despite all the risks they face, they continue to put their lives on the line everyday. His word were simply, "The sun will rise again, evil will not win."

Because of this personal tragedy Ella is grateful for her faith and for her blue family. Many of them knew her brother-in-law and his life and death has caused them all to connect more and grow stronger.

After twenty-five years of standing by her Officer through all the highs and lows of the Law Enforcement life, Ella shares her wisdom with other wives behind the blue.

A Wife's Advice

1. Strengthen your Weakness: Sometimes, we're afraid to admit, or show our weaknesses that we have to deal with in our Law Enforcement marriages and families. We want to be the "hero-wife" or "strong-wife", when in truth, we just may feel weak. It's okay to feel week but we also need to take the time to strengthen our weaknesses. I do this by hanging out with happy, joyful people, it encourages and strengthens me.

2. Don't doubt your calling as an Officer's wife: God can use any one of us. We just have to be obedient and slightly brave at times.

3. Keep your finances in order: Time flies, babies come, retirement comes, and you want to be ready for that. Don't be tied to the "toys", or try to "keep up with the Jones."

4. Let God be your peace: After being brought to my knees in stress and now in grief, I have seen no other way to survive this Law Enforcement life, than to have a personal relationship with Jesus. The Bible says in a simple verse, "For God so loved the world, that he gave his only son, Jesus, that whosoever believes in him, should not perish, but have eternal life." (John 3:16)

5. My husband knows Jesus and so did my brother-in-law. The moment he died, he was in heaven at the feet of Jesus, complete and healed. That was my immediate peace in a horrible storm. A peace that could be yours too.

A Wife's Prayer

Dear God,

I know the reality. I know that injury or death can happen, yet I still choose to walk this journey with my husband. I still choose to stand beside him, to support him and love him especially when it gets hard. Thank you for believing in my Officer and for believing in me. May every aspect of our lives, the blue life included, bring great honor and glory to you always.

My Thoughts:

And that about wraps it up. God is strong, and he wants you strong. So take everything the Master has set out for you, well-made weapons of the best materials. And put them to use so you will be able to stand up to everything the Devil throws your way.

~Ephesians 6:10

WHAT I'VE LEARNED

When I had prayed for what, if any writing project God might have for me this summer, this book would have been the last possible thing I would have thought of. But now as I come to the end, I can't begin to explain how happy I am that God chose this book to be the summer project. If He had not, I would never have had the opportunity or inclination to connect with such amazing women, all like me, married to a Law Enforcement Officer.

One of the most profound moments for me in this journey was the night I was asked to meet six wives whom I had connected with via email, to contribute to this book. I had met with one of them once prior but the other five ladies I did not know at all. The ladies were all for the idea of supporting me and this project but before they opened up about some of their experiences of being a wife of an Officer, they wanted to meet me and find out what I was all about.

I was set to meet a group of women I didn't know, at a restaurant I'd never heard of, to talk about a subject, I had never really spoken of. When I walked into the restaurant, I was nervous. I sat down at the reserved table and as the ladies arrived they greeted each other with warmth and familiarity. And they greeted me the same way. There are two things the ladies who were there that night do not know, but will once they read this book in its entirety. One being that during the first fifteen minutes that I was there a huge part of me wanted to run away and hide. My instinct to "not talk about being a Law Enforcement wife" was in full gear and as crazy as this may sound, sitting with them, I felt vulnerable and exposed. But I had to suck up my nervous feelings because after all, I was asking these ladies to open up a bit of their own life and share with me and all the many readers of this book. Eventually, my nerves settled and I sat back and really listened as these six wives laughed, talked, connected, and discussed the life of a Law Enforcement wife.

This particular group of women along with other women they knew, had formed a Law Enforcement Officers Wives Bible Study/Support Group a year prior and they were all better for it. I honestly felt speechless at moments as I listened to them talk about their life as blue sisters. They weren't leaving out the "blue life" in the conversations as I was accustomed to doing, they were in it together and the camaraderie and support was evident. Sitting around the table together, the group of women were shocked to learn that in seventeen years, that dinner with them was my first real interaction with other wives of Officers.

The second thing the ladies who were there that night do not know is that when I gave each of them a hug and said goodbye, thanking them for taking the time to meet with me, I got in my car, called a dear friend and cried all the way home while talking to her about these amazing sisters in blue.

I was overcome with emotions. Connecting with

like-minded women who completely understood the life I have been living for nearly two decades, without having to explain it and feeling their genuine support of love for one another was overwhelming.

While being the wife of my Officer has been good all these years, it has not been without challenge. The biggest challenge at times has been the feeling of no one understanding this crazy life you must embrace when your husband is called to be a Law Enforcement Officer.

I will never forget that night, meeting with other wives behind the blue. Without knowing it, they ministered to something deep in my soul. If this book can encourage just one wife who might otherwise never connect with other blue wives due to the private nature of being a part of Law Enforcement, then this summer project has been well worth every moment.

RESOURCES

Here are a few good resources for wives behind the blue that I came across in my research. New resources seem to be popping every day so let this list be you starting point for growth in your journey.

BOOKS:

I Love a Cop by Dr. Ellen Kirschman
Emotional Survival for Law Enforcement by Dr. Kevin M. Gilmartin
Bullets in the Washing Machine by Melissa Littles
Because I'm Suitable – The Journey of a Wife on Duty by Allison Uribe
Cuffs & Coffee by Allison Uribe
CHiP on my Shoulder – How to Love Your Cop with Attitude by Victoria Newman
Survival Guide for Police Wives by Kristi Neace
Above the Fray by Kristi Neace
The Crazy Lives of Police Wives by Caroyln Whiting and Carolyn LaRoche
Behind the Badge - 365 Devotions for America's Law Enforcement by Adam Davis

WEBSITES:

How 2 Love Your Cop
www.how2loveyourcop.com
National Police Wives Association
www.nationalpolicewivesassocation.org
National Alliance for Law Enforcement Support
www.nalestough.org
Blue Line Wives
www.bluelinewives.com

FACEBOOK:

Wives On Duty Ministries
National Police Wives Association
Badge of Hope Ministries
The Blue Line Wives
Thin Blue Line Wife

BLOGS:

Suddenly Cop Wife
www.suddenlycopwife.blogspot.com
Happy Police Wife
www.1happypolicewife.blogspot.com
The Police Wife's Life
www.thepolicewifelifeblog.com/blog
Walking the Thin Blue Line
www.walkingthethinblueline.com/blog
Police Wives of America
www.policewivesofamerica.org/blog

About the Author

Monica Amor has been a Law Enforcement Officer's Wife for almost two decades. and is passionate about sharing hope, faith, encouragement, and a bit of wisdom to her blue line sisters and all others who come her way.

Follow on Facebook: @Wives Behind The Blue

Also Available From

WordCrafts Press

www.wordcrafts.net

Made in the USA
Lexington, KY
09 January 2019